THE
POWER
OF GOING
ALL-IN

THE POWER OF GOING ALL-IN

SECRETS FOR SUCCESS IN BUSINESS, LEADERSHIP, AND LIFE

BRANDON BORNANCIN
SEAMLESS.AI

WILEY

Published by John Wiley & Sons, Inc., Hoboken, New Jersey.
Published simultaneously in Canada.

For general information on our other products and services or for technical support, please contact our Customer Care Department within the United States at (800) 762-2974, outside the United States at (317) 572-3993 or fax (317) 572-4002.

Wiley also publishes its books in a variety of electronic formats. Some content that appears in print may not be available in electronic formats. For more information about Wiley products, visit our web site at www.wiley.com.

Library of Congress Cataloging-in-Publication Data:

Names: Bornancin, Brandon, author.
Title: The power of going all-in : secrets for success in business,
    leadership, and life / Brandon Bornancin.
Description: Hoboken, New Jersey : Wiley, [2024] | Includes index.
Identifiers: LCCN 2023048986 (print) | LCCN 2023048987 (ebook) | ISBN
    9781394196180 (hardback) | ISBN 9781394196197 (adobe pdf) | ISBN
    9781394196203 (epub)
Subjects: LCSH: Leadership.
Classification: LCC HD57.7 .B676 2024 (print) | LCC HD57.7 (ebook) | DDC
    658.4/092—dc23/eng/20231207
LC record available at https://lccn.loc.gov/2023048986
LC ebook record available at https://lccn.loc.gov/2023048987

Cover Design: Seamless.AI

SKY10064680_011224

This book is dedicated to all the incredible leaders, managers, mentors, and coaches I've had the privilege to work with.

You've taught me everything I know about the power of going all-in, and I'm truly grateful to share these lessons with others.

To all the readers striving to become the best you can be to positively impact others, you are the true heroes.

This book will help you and all the people you serve achieve greatness.

You can do anything with
The Power of Going All-In!

Contents

Introduction

No matter who you are, success in life requires going all-in. Think about it for a second. Think about anything great you ever achieved. Was it because you put in half of your time, energy, and resources to get it done? Or did you achieve massive success because you gave it everything you had and you went all-in to make it happen?

I make a point every year to do an inventory and reflect on all my successes and failures, and I noticed a pattern. Anything great I've ever achieved in my life was because I went all-in. And anything I failed at in my life was because I *didn't* go all-in.

In fact, every time I failed, there was always something I could've done, learned, applied, or tried that would've changed the outcome of that situation for the better. If you're tired of getting mediocre results, then going all-in and applying everything I'm about to teach you in this book is going to help you make your dreams a reality.

In *The Power of Going All-In*, I'm thrilled to share with you my strategies to change your life and transform your success in business, leadership, and life. This book is not just a guide; it's a daily mentor, a companion, and a resource available to you every step of the way as you work toward becoming the best leader you can be.

My name is Brandon Bornancin, and I am honored to be your guide on this transformative journey. Throughout my career, I've worn many hats. I started a company with just $1,000 and turned it into a $100,000,000 business in just four years. Along the way, I've hired and managed hundreds of people. I survived the rocky ups and downs of corporate America selling for big companies like IBM and Google. I've written multiple best-selling books, and I've had the honor of speaking globally about how to win in both business and life.

With each role, I've had the privilege of learning valuable lessons that helped take my performance and the results of everyone I worked with to unprecedented levels. These experiences ultimately shaped my understanding of what it takes to effectively lead a team and help everyone reach their greatest potential. However, out of all the lessons I've learned, the most important of them all is. . .

THE POWER OF GOING ALL-IN

I remember when I started my career, I didn't think I had the skills, the knowledge, or the motivation to lead others to achieve great things. Hell, I didn't believe that I could achieve much of anything myself.

Then one day I decided to stop listening to the doubt and the fear, and instead I went all-in with my leadership. I committed myself wholeheartedly to my team's growth. Once I went all-in, I was able to help a few people become better than they were when they started their positions. Eventually, those few people turned into dozens and later hundreds. But all the success started the day I decided to leverage the power of going all-in, and you can do the same!

It's your responsibility to go all-in for the people you serve, for your family, and for yourself because they are all counting on you.

Everyone in this world, whether you believe it or not, is a leader. And as a leader, your role is not limited to driving strategy or ensuring execution. As a top leader, it's your job to help your employees achieve more than they ever believed they could achieve.

You have to encourage people's dreams, help them overcome their obstacles, and remain resilient during difficult times. *The Power of Going All-In* is about making sure that, no matter what, you have the tools to help your team feel secure, supported, and energized because you have their back no matter what, every step of the way.

GREAT LEADERS VS. BAD BOSSES

Throughout my career, I've worked for some incredible leaders. And I've had the misfortune of working for some terrible bosses.

The leaders who maximized my potential taught me what was required to succeed. They held me accountable and helped me overcome any challenges I faced both professionally and personally.

In contrast, the terrible bosses I've worked for nearly destroyed my potential. You know a bad boss when you see one. It typically starts with them demanding that you call them your boss. Then they avoid showing any appreciation and instead give you nothing but negative feedback on your performance. They rarely offer any ideas or strategies to get better. They're disorganized. They don't even know how to do the job they are asking of you. Instead of lending a helping hand and leading from the trenches, bad bosses micromanage their team's every move and fire them if they don't hit their goals.

No one wants to work for a bad boss, but we've all had them. Bad bosses are the worst. But what's the core difference between great leaders and bad bosses?

There are many factors that make exceptional leaders great, which we'll discuss in detail. But if you look at the top 1% of leaders across any company or industry, the one trait they all have in common is that they leverage the power of going all-in.

WHAT DOES IT MEAN TO GO ALL-IN?

"Going all-in" or "all-in leadership" (I use both interchangeably throughout this book) is all at once a mindset and a way of life. It's an unwavering commitment to excellence and a relentless pursuit of growth.

The power of going all-in pushes against leadership norms like micromanaging and turning your team into mindless robots. Instead, going all-in empowers companies to become the unstoppable leaders of tomorrow.

Anyone going all-in refuses to settle for anything average or ordinary and instead strives to help their team achieve the extraordinary.

Going all-in is about channeling your time, energy, and resources into a purpose bigger than yourself and helping your employees take their careers to the next level.

Going all-in encompasses the following core characteristics:

- **Massive goals:** All-in leaders never settle for average, and they aren't afraid to set massive, ambitious goals for themselves, their team, and their business. They're always ready to put in the effort to make their dreams a reality and take their company to new heights.
- **Positivity:** No matter the obstacle, people who are all-in take a glass-half-full approach to everything in life and stay positive at all costs. This positivity makes the biggest challenges seem minor, and it turns every setback into an opportunity for growth. The relentless positivity of all-in leaders is the momentum that pushes their team forward.
- **Coachability:** Regardless of how much experience an all-in leader has, they never get a big ego or think they're too good to learn anymore. Instead, leveraging the power of going all-in is all about staying humble, coachable, hungry to learn, and eager to improve.
- **Strong work ethic:** All-in leaders aren't afraid to get their hands dirty and put in good old-fashioned hard work. Hustle beats talent when talent doesn't hustle, and an all-in leader is always the first to show up at the office and the last to leave because they understand that hard work is the magic behind the greatest successes.
- **Whatever it takes (WIT):** When there's a goal, all-in leaders are willing to do whatever it takes to make it happen. Whether they have to put in extra hours, invest more money, or get down in the trenches with their employees, all-in leaders give everything they've got to make the impossible possible.
- **No excuses:** All-in leaders have zero tolerance for excuses for themselves or their teammates because excuses are distractions that

get in the way of improvement. When you're an all-in leader trying to make the world a better place, there's no room for excuses.

- **Extreme ownership:** When the team wins, all-in leaders give all the credit. And when things don't go as planned, they take full ownership of the mistakes and 100% of the blame.
- **Unshakable commitment:** All-in leaders possess an unbreakable commitment to their vision. They are fully invested in their pursuits and willing to go above and beyond to make their goals happen.
- **Fearless resilience:** Going all-in means embracing failure as a stepping stone to success. All-in leaders bounce back from setbacks, learn from their mistakes, and use adversity as fuel to propel themselves forward. Their resilience allows them to navigate through challenges with unwavering determination.
- **Limitless passion:** All-in leaders understand that passion is a powerful catalyst for extraordinary achievements, so they are driven by an insatiable passion for what they do. Their enthusiasm is infectious, and they're great at fostering a collective sense of purpose.
- **Courageous vision:** Top leaders have a bold vision for the future of their team. They have the skills to not only articulate this vision clearly but motivate others to join them on their journey. Their courageous vision ultimately becomes an essential compass, guiding their decisions, their actions, and the people they serve.
- **Continuous growth mindset:** All-in leaders are lifelong learners. They actively seek opportunities for personal and professional development. Never content, they embrace constructive feedback, seek out mentors, and always strive to expand their knowledge and skill sets.

When all-in leadership takes root, the impact is profound! Organizations experience exponential growth, innovation, and a culture of excellence. All-in leaders create an environment where individuals are encouraged to think bigger, reach new heights, and challenge the status quo.

While there are countless benefits to your company and your team, on a personal level, going all-in can unlock your true potential because it forces you to tap into your hidden strengths and unleash your creativity. All-in leadership enables you to live a life of purpose and fulfillment, knowing that you are making a lasting impact on the world around you.

WHY GOING ALL-IN IS REQUIRED FOR SUCCESS

The only way for you and your team to become the best is by going all-in. Going all-in is not an option; it's a requirement. It's necessary. It's imperative. By embracing the principles in this book, leaders like you can create a ripple effect of inspiration, trust, and innovation.

All-in leaders are the ones who change the world. They set the bar high, challenging others to reach extraordinary heights. So, as a leader, embrace the power of going all-in, and witness the transformational impact it has on your team, your company, your family, and your legacy.

Going all-in is not for the faint of heart. It requires vision and an unwavering commitment to excellence. But blazing a trail in your industry and building a lasting legacy are rewards that make it all worthwhile.

Anyone who changed the world and became the best they can be went all-in. Now it's your time to go all-in and accomplish the same.

HOW THIS BOOK IS STRUCTURED

The Power of Going All-In consists of 365 leadership secrets and strategies. These secrets are divided into four parts. Each part contains three chapters, and each chapter contains roughly 30–31 secrets. You may notice that I discuss some themes and secrets more than once throughout the book. And that's because with more involved topics such as coaching or servant leadership, instead of sharing just one secret that only scratches the surface, I revisit these themes to delve deeper and to drive home key points that you may not get the first time around.

The four parts of *The Power of Going All-In* are broken down as follows:

- **Part 1: The Principles for Going All-In** provides you with the groundwork to build a strong team built for maximum success. We tackle how to develop a scalable mission and vision that gives your team purpose and direction. We'll go over repeatable recruiting tactics, from key traits to look for in interviews to hiring and putting together a dream team. We'll also look at onboarding strategies that get your people ramped up and on a clear career path ASAP. This part additionally provides strategies to maximize your team's performance. The concepts in this part are the essential building blocks for becoming a leader who is all-in from the start.

- **Part 2: The Strategies for Building High-Performing Teams** covers the best tactics for harnessing tenacity in the face of failure, as well as problem-solving as a team. No matter how big or small your department KPIs are, this part will share strategies to help your people set ambitious personal and professional goals and achieve them utilizing an all-in mindset. Moreover, when you complete this part, you will perfect the art of leadership communication, from active listening tips to setting clear expectations and becoming an expert at having tough conversations that hold others accountable.

- **Part 3: The Keys to Unlocking Your Team's Potential** is all about building trust because teams perform their best when there is a culture rooted in trust. This part covers tactics to foster buy-in and collaboration. We will also go over how you can build trust among your employees and your inner circle of peers by getting down in the trenches with them. I'll then show you how to create an environment where your people feel comfortable coming to you with problems so you not only can help solve them but also provide them with the autonomy to get creative, test new strategies, and drive results.

- **Part 4: The Secrets to Developing the Next Generation of Leaders** teaches you all the frameworks for promoting diversity, inclusion, and empowerment among your team. We'll look at strategies to effectively prioritize your largest projects and tasks month to month. This section also includes secrets to drawing the maximum talent from every personality and work style. Lastly, in looking to the future, I will cover how to coach your team to execute beyond their current position and take on future leadership roles. To scale, you need new leaders to take on new responsibilities, and that is what Part 4 is all about.

DAILY READING AND DAILY ACTION

The Power of Going All-In was written as an easy-to-use actionable guide. Each day, you will be introduced to a new lesson that will challenge your thinking and help you make a positive impact on others.

As you implement these secrets, I am confident you will witness remarkable transformations within yourself and your team. You just have to commit to daily action and work toward improving at least 1% each day.

One of the guiding principles to going all-in is to improve by at least 1% every day. What this principle dictates is that no matter what industry you're in, if you strive to generate at least 1% more results than you did the day before—and if you consistently improve by 1% every day for the next year—you will end the year 37x better than when you started. Need more proof?

Let's say you're a leader of a $1,000,000 business. If you increase your results by 1% every day, you and your team can grow the business to $37,000,000 within a year! That's the power of compounding interest, and that's why this book contains 365 secrets. Learn a secret a day. Execute it. End the year 37x better than when you first picked up this book.

While the book is structured so you can explore one secret each day for the next year, feel free to read it in a way that best suits your needs. That means you can read *The Power of Going All-In* from cover to cover in a few sittings or refer to a secret whenever you feel stuck or need inspiration. It's also OK to skip a secret if it covers a topic you've mastered. Just trust your instincts and spend time on the secrets that will drive the greatest results or help you make the greatest transformation.

However you read *The Power of Going All-In*, remember your leadership journey is not a sprint but a marathon. This book is ultimately designed to motivate you to keep going when the path seems difficult. The managers and leaders who go all-in never give up; there is always a way. There is always a solution. You just have to find it.

CLOSING

I believe that leadership is a privilege, and with that privilege comes the responsibility to serve others, help others, and inspire change.

Going all-in is more than just a title; it's a commitment: a commitment to your team, to your family, and, most importantly, to yourself. It's a commitment to become the best leader you can be in all facets of your life, both professionally and personally.

By picking up this book, you have already demonstrated your commitment to excellence, and you've made your team's success your top priority over anything else. For that, I commend you!

I am excited about what lies ahead as you embark on this transformative adventure because *The Power of Going All-In* will change your life forever for the better.

Before we begin, consider leaving a review about your thoughts on *The Power of Going All-In* here:

https://www.amazon.com/All-Leadership-Give-Everything-Succeed/dp/1394196180

When you write a review, you help increase the exposure of this book so more people hear about it, pick it up, and start working on their own leadership transformation. Everyone wins!

Thank you in advance, and now, let's start your all-in leadership journey and dive into Part I!

Your success is my success,
Brandon Bornancin
CEO & Founder
www.seamless.ai
www.brandonbornancin.com

PART I

THE PRINCIPLES
FOR GOING ALL-IN

MONTH 1

MISSION, VISION, AND ACCOUNTABILITY

#1

INVEST DAILY IN BECOMING A GREAT LEADER

It's important for you to practice the leadership secrets in this book every day and invest in becoming the best leader you can be for yourself and your team. Leadership is always changing, and the work is never done. You can always learn new strategies and execute new plans to increase your team's success.

Leaders who don't bother to continuously improve see these same problems come up over and over again:

- **Busywork:** Employees work on things that don't matter to the company mission or bottom line.
- **Volatility:** Team goals seem to change with the weather, creating stress and uncertainty.
- **Confusion:** People don't understand why they are working on certain tasks.
- **Unrealistic goals:** Goals are too abstract and never accomplished.
- **Zero buy-in:** You struggle to get the buy-in on the initiatives you need, and you don't know why.

Look to see if your team is dealing with any of these common problems and work to nip them in the bud.

#2

OWN THE VISION

The dictionary defines *vision* as "the act of seeing or the power of seeing." All-in leaders create the vision, explain the vision, passionately own the vision, and drive the vision to completion.

In fact, I would say that an all-in leader has an uncanny ability to envision their team's potential even when things look bleak.

- Vision inspires the team.
- Vision helps teams work through obstacles and move forward on the journey to success.
- Vision gives purpose and meaning to the work people do.
- Vision helps the team crush goals with efficiency.

It's all about the vision, the values, the data, and the people.

Own the vision and drive the vision to completion.

#3

BE CLEAR ABOUT YOUR VISION

If you want your team to work cohesively to crush projects, start incorporating statements of work (SOWs) in your projects. An SOW is an outline of all the important components of a project that your team will need to complete the project in a timely manner.

Here are some core parts to include in an SOW to give your team a clear sense of the vision for a project:

- The key components of the project as well as assigned owners.
- What the project doesn't entail. (Maybe later down the line, you anticipate your project requiring the attention of product development or recruiting. But for now, this project just needs your team's attention. Be clear about this and *all* the parameters of the project.)
- What the final product should look like.

Once you've come up with an SOW, run it by your higher-ups to see if there's anything worth adding.

Then you're off to the races with a concise, actionable document that holds every individual contributor accountable and gives your team momentum.

#4
YOU WORK FOR YOUR TEAM

As a CEO, a team manager, a business operator, etc. it's crazy to expect your employees to work as much as you do. It's *your* company or team, so of course your employees won't care as much as you or "love the work" as much as you do.

If you want to be an effective leader, you have to give your employees everything you've got. Give, give, give, and then give some more to maximize their potential with no expectations of anything in return.

You're going to have much more success if you set these expectations up front with your team and always give them the support they need.

#5
BE THE LEADER EMPLOYEES WANT TO WORK FOR

Candidates don't choose a job. They choose a great leader to work for.

And employees don't stay at a job for nothing. They stay because they have a leader who supports their growth and is always willing to do whatever it takes to maximize their success.

Be the leader who people want to work for.

#6

MAKE THEM BETTER

It's your job as a great leader to make sure you bring everyone you work with up to another level.

Wherever an employee is at performance-wise when you hire them, your objective is to make them better. Take someone good on the team and make them excellent. Take someone on the team who's excellent and turn them into a rock star.

If you can master this leadership principle and execute it every day, everyone will want to work for you.

#7

EVERYONE WINS WHEN YOU GIVE YOUR HELP SELFLESSLY

While there are millions of people in the workforce, they all can be categorized into three different work styles.

- The selfless people who always sacrifice their time and their talent for the betterment of their team and their company
- The "tit-for-tat" people who keep tabs on everything and only give as much as they receive
- The self-centered people who take without giving anything of value in return

To be clear, all three types of people can be successful; however, there are limits to your success when you constantly take without reciprocating or when you play "tit for tat."

When you play "tit for tat," you're only helping your team become as successful as the help that is given to you. When you are self-centered, you create enemies as you're the only person who reaps any benefits. When you selflessly give your mentorship and your guidance, you gain allies, everybody wins, and you drive results month to month, quarter to quarter, and year to year.

#8
FIND THE TRIANGLE BALANCE

Leadership must find the right balance of three core pillars that I call the Triangle Balance:

- **Directive:** Leaders set the goals and encourage employees to work together to develop the strategy and execution to achieve them. Accountability is crucial to the success of this pillar.
- **Supportive:** Leaders check in with employees and ask questions like these: What's going well with your journey to success? What do you need help with professionally or personally to get there? How can I help unblock anything standing in your way?
- **Contributory:** Leaders must give everything they've got to maximize their team's success. The greatest leaders pour themselves into others. They constantly think, "What can I do to help my employees achieve their goals smarter, better, faster, cheaper, and easier than ever before? What strategies, execution plans, or problem-solving can I offer to help you succeed?"

#9
ALWAYS SHOWCASE AARI

A core framework for all-in leadership is the acronym AARI, which stands for the following:

- **Availability:** Ensure that your team knows you are there to help them whenever they need it most.

- **Approachability:** Showcase that you are eager to help team members overcome their biggest problems, achieve their biggest desires, and make every year their biggest and best yet.
- **Responsiveness:** When a team member asks for help or your input, give it to them right away, ideally within a few hours of their request (if it's possible).
- **Investment:** People need leaders who will do whatever it takes to help them improve to become the best version of themselves. Invest in growing the success of your team daily.

#10
UNLEASH YOUR TENACITY

The essential skill every world-class leader needs to thrive is tenacity. Tenacity can be so crucial because it's the quality that will see you through the most challenging situations. It's the thing that will motivate you to keep moving forward when failures and setbacks happen. Tenacity is not just the refusal to give up or the willingness to see things through to the end, but it's also a conviction that you need to have in yourself.

To be a more tenacious leader, you need to know that you can do anything you set your mind to.

If tenacity isn't your strength, start writing the previous statement down on paper at the beginning and end of every day as a reminder. Read it out loud to yourself every single day until you start believing it. And when you start honing your mental endurance, you'll unlock your full tenacity and be able to go through any fires.

#11

DON'T SIT AROUND WAITING

You can't create something valuable by sitting around waiting. Management gets easier when you realize that the leaders who you admire are just like you. The only difference is, they did whatever it took to get started, and they stayed inquisitive, positive, coachable, and hard-working.

Impactful leaders have the choice to get started or to sit around and never begin. But they always choose the former because nothing great ever gets done by doing nothing.

#12

FREE YOURSELF FROM THE NEED FOR RESPECT

Great leaders don't care about being called a manager. Great leaders don't care about having their team "respect" them. Great leaders don't care about being higher up on the pyramid than others.

Great leaders care about only one thing: doing whatever it takes to help their team accomplish their dreams.

You can't just expect your team to respect you because of your title. You must earn their respect by investing in them and helping them succeed. You only succeed as a leader when your team succeeds.

#13

KNOW YOUR UPSIDE AND DOWNSIDE

To become a great leader, it is extremely important to always calculate your upside and downside in all facets of your management. Business is a very strict risk versus reward game, and the people who know their numbers take all the rewards, while the people who don't know the numbers lose everything.

In management, you must understand the numbers. You have to know what is invested, how much is at risk, and what you must be OK with losing if the risk doesn't produce the reward you were looking for. The only way to do this is to hypothesize the upside, the downside, and the probability of success for every project, and once the project is completed, track the performance data.

As you track the data, if the numbers are meeting or exceeding projections, you can continue to invest in the project. If things are going poorly and you aren't seeing the results, you have to stop investing in the project or shut it down as quickly as possible.

As long as you know your numbers and track the upside and downside, you will be in a great position to continuously optimize operations.

#14

HOLD TEAM MASTERMINDS

This secret is specifically for leaders who work remotely. If this is you, I want you to make it a priority every quarter to get together with your team in person and host a mastermind.

A mastermind is an event where your team gathers together to work on projects, collaborate, brainstorm, network, and just catch up.

Masterminds may seem trivial and not necessary, but don't underestimate the power of working together in person because this is the time where your team can really overcome long-standing challenges, uncover crucial goals, and identify opportunities for improvement. In a world where a lot of people work remotely, try to get your team together in person at least quarterly regardless of the time it takes or the cost.

When I run team or leadership masterminds, we like to discuss the following:

- Big projects we are trying to accomplish (progress, obstacles, etc.)
- Team members' professional goals
- Team members' personal goals
- Biggest professional challenges and problems
- Biggest personal challenges and problems
- How to help

Every quarter, give a supercharge to team morale with a mastermind.

#15
MAKE THE CALL AND ROLL

Most decisions I've made as a leader were based on research. I'd identify a problem, research how to solve it, and then come up with a solution to execute right away. Instead of wasting time asking the team what they thought, I just rolled it out and explained, "This is what we are going to do, and here is why. Do you have any other alternatives to address this issue?"

I've helped our team make tens of millions of dollars because of different calls I made that worked out in our favor. When people in my network advised against it, in my gut I knew it was exactly what we needed to do to solve a problem or get to the next level, so I went with my instincts and took the shot.

Now it's important to point out that whatever strategies, projects, or recommendations you roll with, you have to take full ownership even if they end up being failures. But if you are OK with taking ownership, then follow your gut. If it works out, fantastic! If it doesn't, you gained experience to make a smarter decision next time.

If you know that waiting around for a consensus isn't going to be feasible, then make the call and roll.

#16
CELEBRATE THE WINS OF YOUR TEAM EVERY DAY

Celebrating your team's accomplishments (big or small) leads to long-term success. Celebrating the wins of your team every day creates camaraderie. Celebrating the wins of the team every day helps inspire your people to do more, be more, and achieve more than they thought they could.

Encourage everyone on your team to share their wins and celebrate each other. The way we've done this with every department at Seamless.AI is by creating a "GONG" or a Wins channel on Slack where anyone can post a win they accomplished.

- Our sales development representative (SDR) sales team posts every time someone books a meeting.
- Our customer success team posts every time they save an account or upsell an account.
- Our collections team posts every time they collect an unpaid invoice.
- Our HR team posts every time they book an interview or get an offer letter signed.
- Our marketing team posts the new users, demos, and sales they generate every day.
- Our engineering team celebrates when bugs or new features are pushed out.

When the win gets posted, the entire company celebrates. Inspire your team to post their wins every day.

#17
TEACH THE TEAM GRATITUDE

Instead of waiting until your team scores a win to be grateful, teach your team to express gratitude every day.

I recommend having each employee keep a gratitude journal to list anything they are grateful for that day, big or small (a great meal, a great co-worker, etc.). Additionally, teach your team to change the way they perceive work.

Instead of looking at work as something they "have to do," they should look at work as something that they "get to do." They get to transform people's lives with the product or service they provide, and that's something to truly be grateful for.

It's so important to have gratitude along the journey to success because these small gestures add up to a paradigm shift. Gratitude allows you to see the best in everything around you, and it unlocks the fullness of life.

#18
BECOME A VISIONARY LEADER

As a leader, you always have to think 10 steps ahead so you have a competitive edge.

To become a more visionary leader, you must

- **Be realistic:** Thinking you can't get started on your vision until you have whatever ridiculously priced tool (you think you need) will kill your progress. And expecting to achieve 10× goals in a short amount of time will kill your progress. So be realistic with your vision and think about what you currently have at your fingertips. How can you maximize the value you're getting out of what you already have?

- **Do an inventory of wins and losses:** Go through past wins and failures, and do an inventory of the winning habits, strategies, frameworks, and approaches, as well as the bad habits and missteps. Replicate the behaviors that led to victories and eliminate the missteps that slowed your team's progress in the past.

As a visionary leader, it should be your goal to get your team so excited about the future you envision for the company that they're ready to bust through a wall to get to it faster!

#19
LEADERSHIP IS A PRIVILEGE

Many leaders feel that having a management position is their God-given right. They act as if they are better than those who work for them. I'm here to give you a reality check and remind you that leadership is a privilege, not a right.

Leadership is never owned; it is rented, and the rent is due every day to serve your people to achieve greater levels of success in the game of life.

Great leaders are humble and obsessed with serving their team, not being served by their team. Leaders are accountable for the success and livelihood of dozens to thousands of people. Leaders' actions and decisions impact a large and diverse community.

Always remember that leadership is a *privilege*, not a right. When you are a leader, your influence can affect the trajectory of people's personal and professional lives.

#20

GREAT LEADERSHIP SPREADS LIKE WILDFIRE

One of the most amazing things about being a leader is positively impacting the people you lead. The people you lead have the potential to reach hundreds of thousands of people and kick-start game-changing ideas and conversations.

Since your impact as a leader can spread far and wide above you and those around you, give it your all. Push yourself as hard as possible to serve, to share brilliant ideas, and to inspire.

You have the opportunity to lead others to create something that changes the world. Start that fire that spreads new intelligence, ideas, and dreams far and wide!

#21

DEVELOP THE LEADERS OF THE FUTURE

The ultimate euphoria for an all-in leader is to help their people maximize their success, grow in their careers, and get to the next level. By helping your employees become the best leaders and bosses of the future, you learn from them and you both maximize your success.

In fact, that's how this book got started. I wanted to train my team, so I wrote these secrets as a leadership development plan, and they were so impactful that I decided to share them with the world.

Luckily for you, if you want to help your employees grow in their leadership abilities, you don't need to create a book. Just give them a copy of this book or create your own simple playbook and start teaching the team these principles and secrets to being a great leader.

#22
HELP YOUR PEOPLE SET GOALS

Great managers make their team stronger by helping them set goals.

Help your people set their monthly, quarterly, and annual goals and follow these strategies:

- **Set measurable goals:** Make the goal measurable rather than abstract. This way you and the employee can track progress.
- **Set goals outside of their skill set:** Make sure the goal requires the employee to stretch and learn a skill that's slightly above their current position and abilities. This forces them to hone those leadership skills.
- **Be realistic:** Avoid setting impossible goals. It's great to have high expectations, but you don't want to set a goal so high that the employee can't achieve it. Instead, start with smaller goals and use those tiny victories as momentum for the bigger goals.

#23
WE ARE A TEAM

Teach the people that you lead that you are all on a team. Everyone has one goal and one mission.

I like to tell my team that we are a championship team. If one person on the team struggles, we all struggle. If one person on the team triumphs, we all triumph. We win as a team, and we lose as a team.

Help each other persevere through the struggles, the tribulations, and the challenges. Help each other celebrate the successes, achievements, and wins.

#24

DITCH THE BLAME GAME

It's too easy to blame your lack of success on external factors like a better product or a better manager. Coach your team to quit playing the blame game and to take full responsibility for everything.

The minute you take full ownership for everything good and bad in your life is the minute you are set free to achieve your wildest dreams.

Instead of making excuses, ask your team these questions:

- What are you going to do today to take full responsibility for everything good and bad in your life?
- What are you going to do today to increase your strengths and minimize your weaknesses?
- What are you going to do today to get one step closer to achieving your goals and dreams?

#25

TO BE THE BEST TEAM LEADER, BE FLEXIBLE

This might go against what you've learned, but being a team leader and being uncompromising aren't a good combo. You have to learn to be a team player and bend to meet your team's needs.

If you doubt this advice, I want to point out the following benefits that come with being flexible:

- You learn to be more innovative and resourceful. When you're flexible, no problem can make you sweat, because you're too resourceful to stress. Flexible leaders perfect the art of turning problems into opportunities.

- You learn to empower your people. When you focus on being flexible, you shake off a lot of those selfish impulses that get in the way of serving your team.

With these benefits, learn to bend to the needs and the will of the team, for their greatest success and yours!

#26

MAKE YOUR PEOPLE FEEL IMPORTANT

When you talk to managers, you get the feeling that they are important. When you talk to great leaders, they give you the feeling that you are important.

Make your people feel important.

Your People > You.

#27

UNLOCK YOUR EMPLOYEES' PASSION

At Seamless.AI, one of our mantras is that the work we do isn't something we *have* to do, but something we *get* to do. Every day we connect hundreds of thousands of people to life-changing opportunities. And that's a privilege we don't take for granted.

Your goal as a leader should be to unlock this same drive in your people and get them excited about their work. Before you ever make a request, take these insights into account, and ignite that passion.

Make sure you're clear and specific about exactly what you want. You'd be surprised at how many leaders reach out to an employee with an ask and don't even know what they really want. Think about the things the employee wants the most, and make sure that when you vocalize this request, you speak 100% to what they want.

Unlocking passion is about focusing on what your people want, not what you want.

#28

LIFE PARTNERS NEED TO BE BOUGHT INTO THE MISSION

I've worked with a lot of employees whose partners weren't bought into the mission and vision of the team. When this happens, it ends in absolute disaster.

Eventually, that toxic energy and negative self-talk from the partner will degrade your team member's commitment, positivity, coachability, work ethic, and enthusiasm to maximize their success.

Do whatever it takes to help your team's partners understand the importance of the mission and vision of the company. If they aren't bought in, your team members won't be bought in for long either.

#29

THE ONLY CONSTANT IN LIFE IS CHANGE

Great leaders are constantly adapting to change because change is inevitable.

- Companies change.
- Technology changes.
- People change.
- Problems change.
- Opportunities change.
- Economies change.
- Goals change.

Great leaders are aware of this reality. Instead of staying wedded to the way things are, they adapt. The only way to succeed as a great leader in this ever-changing world is to constantly change with it.

#30

TEACH YOUR TEAM THE PRINCIPLES OF WINNING

Educate your team to surround themselves with people who push them to do better and be better. Educate the team to eliminate all negativity and stay away from any internal team or external team drama as much as possible.

The only thing you want the team to do is set higher goals and have higher motivation. Maintain positive energy throughout the team as much as possible because the goal is to bring out the absolute best in each other no matter what. Become unstoppable together (as a team) and individually (as a contributor).

#31
EVERYONE IS A LEADER

A lot of people think that leadership is all about a management title or directing a big group of people. True leadership is never about authority and power. It's about caring for the people you serve and helping them grow. Anyone in any position can do that.

A leader is someone with a desire to help influence and positively impact others. If you help inspire someone to do something that they thought they couldn't do or if you believed in someone when they didn't believe in themselves, then you are a leader.

If you help serve others, you are a leader. You don't ever need a title to be a leader. We are all leaders.

MONTH 2

BUILDING THE FOUNDATION FOR GREAT HIRING AND ONBOARDING

#1

BECOME GREAT AT RECRUITING AND HIRING

A leader is someone who can build a great team to accomplish goals bigger and faster than others. To do this, you need to be able to recruit, interview, and hire the best talent.

Start studying how to recruit top talent. Analyze what it takes to develop a predictable, repeatable, and scalable interviewing and candidate scoring process. Finalize an approach that is repeatable for hiring and placing top talent on the team.

When you are recruiting and hiring, you want to find people who will increase the overall wisdom of the crowd and the diversity of the crowd. The best ways to do this are by developing your current people and hiring better people in the future who raise everyone up.

#2

HIRE THE PEOPLE TODAY THAT YOU WILL NEED IN THE FUTURE

All those people and resources you need six to nine months from now to hit your plan? Hire these individual contributors right away.

If you hire with the future in mind, you will never have to hire out of desperation or crisis.

#3
APT: ALWAYS PROSPECT TALENT

Great leaders are always on the hunt for top talent. For your most important positions, I recommend prospecting top talent every day.

Today, with many companies going remote, talent has the option to work for anyone anywhere. It's now harder than ever to attract top talent.

This is why you should prospect every day. Also, don't feel pressured to send out 100 outbound messages (email, LinkedIn, etc.) a day. If you have time to send only 5 or 10 messages, that's fine. Just make sure you are consistently getting your company in front of prospects.

While most leaders won't invest the time to prospect passive candidates, if you start prospecting top talent every day, you will find and hire the best much faster than the teams that are doing nothing.

#4
CREATE A REPEATABLE
HIRING PROCESS

To build a team of unstoppable game changers, you need to have a process in place to hire the same quality of people every time, no matter what the position is.

Here are some questions to ask to start putting that hiring system together:

- What are the job requirements?
- What are the interview questions?
- What are the test projects you can have the person complete to validate?

- What questions do you ask references?
- Who needs to interview the candidate?
- What traits are you looking for?
- What experience, skills, and past success are required?
- What is the scorecard to score each candidate the same?

This secret could be an entire book in and of itself; however, with this secret I want to inspire you to start mapping out a predictable, scalable, and repeatable hiring model that anyone can follow internally and execute.

#5

FIND THE ROCK STARS WITH BEHAVIOR-BASED INTERVIEWS

When you're interviewing candidates for roles, everyone gives answers that they know you want to hear. So how do you spot the rock star who is going to help take the company to the next level?

The answer is: behavior-based interview questions.

Not only will behavior-based interview questions give you a better snapshot of a candidate's work experience, but good questions also will give you a sense of how they problem-solve and react to certain situations.

Here are some different behavior-based interview questions you could ask:

- Tell me about a time you had to work under a lot of pressure. How did you respond?
- Can you tell me about a tough problem you faced at work and how you went about solving that problem?

- Can you share with me a time you had to learn a new skill? How did you go about mastering this?
- Tell me about an achievement that you're the proudest of.
- Can you tell me about a time when you didn't achieve the results that you hoped for? How did you respond to this?

#6

HIRE FOR THE THREE I'S

Whenever you're hiring, always pay attention to the three I's.

Initiative

- Does this person learn something and apply what they learn to become the best they can be?
- Does this person take action even if they don't have all the answers?
- If this person doesn't know something, do they make excuses, complain, and quit? Or do they search for the answers and then solve the problem?

Intelligence

- Does this person have self-awareness about their strengths, weaknesses, and so on?
- Does this person showcase a past history of learning, development, and motivation to consistently improve?
- Does this person listen more than they talk? Is this person coachable?

Integrity

- Can I trust this person?
- Does this person have good character?
- Does this person embody the company's mission and core values?

#7

HIRE FOR THIS KEY TRAIT

After interviewing more than 1,000 candidates for various roles at my company, one of the most underrated attributes of top performers that you can't find on a résumé is not the college they attended. It's not their professional experience. It's having a growth mindset.

The best candidates are "growth mindset" individuals who are obsessed with what they can learn, test, discover, improve, and try each day.

Growth mindset individuals are hungry to improve. They have relentless ambition to become the best they can be. And they don't let any obstacles or setbacks hold them back.

When you're looking for talent to build out your team, hire growth mindset–focused individuals.

#8

HIRE PEOPLE WITH ABILITIES YOU CAN'T TEACH

One of the biggest mistakes I see managers make when they're interviewing job candidates is they set their expectations way too high. They have it in their head what the ideal candidate would look like in terms of experience and skills, and they measure every interview based on that dream candidate.

The problem with this approach is that it's unrealistic. Most candidates are going to have some of the qualities you're looking for, but they won't have everything.

So instead of measuring everyone against your dream candidate, make a list of all the qualities you're looking for in a role. Then rank those qualities in order of their difficulty to learn.

The quality that is the easiest to pick up should be a "1," and skills that are hard to teach, such as taking initiative, should be designated with higher numbers. And when you interview, instead of looking for candidates with all the dream qualities, prioritize candidates with more of the qualities that can't be taught. Then when you hire them, train them on the skills that can be learned.

#9

DEVELOP A BUSINESS CASE FOR HIRES

Create a business case template for anyone on your team to hire any new position.

Map out the following categories:

Position

- Who the position reports to:
- Pros of hiring for the position:
- Cons of not hiring for the position (i.e. the cost of inaction):

Investment

- Return on investment (ROI):

When you create a fill-in-the-blank, foolproof template like this that is easy to review, you can help your team ask for the resources they need to hire new employees and buy new tools.

#10

ALWAYS STAY ON THE HUNT FOR TALENT

You always want to build a bench of top talent for future positions you will hire for. This way, when a position opens up, you won't waste time or money searching for a fit because you'll already have a roster of ideal candidates.

Always having a bench of top talent will also help you scale your team more efficiently. I personally prospect 10 people a day for roles I have open or roles I know I want to backfill a bench with. Never stop prospecting top talent.

#11

STOP RECRUITING JUNIOR HIRES

First-time managers often focus on getting junior hires who will work for them and listen to their directions and whose compensation fits an easy-to-afford price tag.

Then later they learn that you really need to hire the best possible people, especially people who are better and more experienced than you.

Great leaders hire the best and pay for the best. People who are better than you raise the current skill set of the team. Find the best, hire the best, and pay for the best. Don't hire junior task completers. Find people who can tell you what you need to do, and do the challenging work that's needed to increase your team's results.

#12

HIRE WITH THE AIM OF LEVELING UP

A major reality a lot of companies have to deal with is high turnover rates. High turnover rates can affect your team's performance as your company struggles to fill open spots.

One of the ways you can cushion the blow of an employee abruptly leaving is giving your people stretch projects where they hone skills that are a level up from their position. Your goal should be to make your employees so well-rounded that when someone leaves, there is little to no impact on your team because there's always an employee who can step up.

One final point to make is that, frequently, when an employee leaves and their exit has a devastating effect on the team, it's because the manager underestimated the value that employee brought to the table.

To avoid this, evaluate your team. Identify the rock stars. Remain aware of the value each team member brings to the table, and do what you can tactically to keep the rock stars from churning.

#13

LOOK FOR A CULTURE ADD

When you are looking to interview and hire new people for the team, don't look for culture "fits." Culture fits blend in and don't do anything to take away from the morale and the culture of a company.

Instead of culture fits, you want to look for "culture adds." These are people who don't just fit in with the company culture, but they add to the culture and give something special to the company that you were desperately missing.

A culture add brings a different perspective, intelligence, experience, talent, and point of view that increases the wisdom and strength of the team so you can accomplish anything and everything.

#14

DEVELOP DEPARTMENT TRANSITION PLANS FAST

For employees who want to transition to new teams and departments, I recommend transitioning them fast. Especially if their performance is satisfactory or above satisfactory. This is because unhappy employees will churn if you don't help them work out a transition plan.

Additionally, you don't want employees in roles they don't want to be in because the work they deliver may not be as great as someone who is all-in on the position.

So for people who want to be moved, work to move them fast to new teams or departments. You never know how their results will change when they're right where they want to be.

#15

THE FIRST 30 TO 90 DAYS ARE INDICATIVE OF THE NEXT FIVE YEARS

When you hire new employees and gauge their performance, the first 90 days will indicate their performance over the next five years. If you aren't that impressed with a team member's performance in the first 30 to 90 days, be prepared for it to rarely change over the next five years.

And if you have a team member who is a rock star, absolutely crushing their goals, be prepared for them to achieve massive success for years to come.

Promote the team members who generate big results in the first 30 to 90 days, and trade team members to other companies who don't generate the results expected.

Keep in mind that if the latter happens, this isn't your fault. They just don't have the experience, motivation, or skill set you need for the specific job. Don't worry, because there are millions of professionals out there who do.

Find the winners for the job and do whatever it takes to maximize their performance.

#16

DO WEEKLY ONBOARD CHECK-INS FOR AN EMPLOYEE'S FIRST MONTH

Employee happiness starts with a great onboarding experience. One of the best ways to create a great onboarding experience is to send a weekly survey for the first four weeks of employment.

Here are two questions I recommended asking in your survey:

- How would you rate your onboarding experience on a scale of 1–10 (10 being the best)?
- What would make it a 10?

Learn from your new employees what is needed to create the best onboarding experience that gives them all the training, support, technology, and direction needed to succeed.

After you run the survey and get the feedback, start taking action to improve the problem areas your people highlight.

#17

DEVELOP AN ONBOARDING SCHEDULE THAT LETS NEW EMPLOYEES SHOWCASE THEIR TALENTS ASAP

When it comes to onboarding, a lot of managers make one of two mistakes. The onboarding process is way too long and you miss out on that valuable window of opportunity where your employee is excited and ready to show their talents, or the onboarding process is way too short and your employee comes out of it unprepared.

You want to find a nice middle ground with your onboarding, where you're giving your employees all they could possibly need to succeed but also taking advantage of their fresh "outsider's" perspective early on.

An onboarding schedule that finds the middle ground would ideally be three months and look something like this:

- **Month 1:** Teach your new employee the ins and outs of your company's culture (mission, vision, origin story) and give them an opportunity to meet the leaders at the organization.
- **Month 2:** Give your new employee a project to work on that focuses on reinvigorating some aspect of the company. It could be the team, the product, you name it. Give them the freedom to complete the project taking whatever approach they want to take.
- **Month 3:** Now that you've had time to figure out your new employee's strengths and growth opportunities, focus on making sure they get settled in the right team, department, or unit. If they're not a good fit for your team but they are clearly talented and will make great contributions to the company, just move them to where they would be a perfect fit.

#18

HOLD REGULAR ONE-ON-ONES AND LET YOUR EMPLOYEE LEAD THE CONVERSATION

Not every manager has regular "one-on-ones" with their team, but these meetings are key to your employees' success, the team's success, and the success of the company.

If you're a new manager, you might be wondering, what exactly is a one-on-one? A one-on-one is your chance to check in with your employees on an individual basis for 25 to 30 minutes. A one-on-one allows you and the employee to connect and see their progress on key goals. It's also an opportunity to work on "stuck-ons."

Even though you are the manager, these meetings should be all about the employee—the priorities at work that they think are important to discuss, the wins they want to share, and the issues they want guidance on.

To get the most out of your meeting time, here are some sample questions you can include in your calendar invite for the one-on-one:

- What goals do you have?
- How was your progress toward these goals during the past week? What wins are you most proud of?
- Are you dealing with any blockers?
- How am I doing? Any feedback for me?
- What else would you like to discuss?

Before the meeting, have the employee document and answer these questions. After the meeting, have your employee summarize the major takeaways from the discussion and share them with you for the sake of accountability. I recommend doing one-on-ones bi-weekly. But however frequently you choose to do them, make sure you don't skip one-on-one time with your employees.

One of the biggest causes for employee churn is management's failure to properly support their people. So, try to always make your one-on-ones top priority so you can help your employees reach their goals.

#19

BUILD A NEW-HIRE ORIENTATION TEMPLATE

During your one-on-ones with new hires, start things off on the right foot with this template. These questions are based on common questions new hires ask during their first week.

General

Get to know each other outside of just work!

- What do you like to do in your free time?
- What's something interesting you've accomplished?

Team Operations

Lay out how the team operates and where to find important information.

- What is the team's recurring meeting cadence?
- Where are processes documented?
- What tools does the team use, and what do they use them for?

Communication

Walk your new hire through the standard communication channels used by the team.

- Where do team members flag urgent matters?
- What time of the day does your new hire do their best work?

30-60-90

Walk your new hire through their onboarding plan for the first 30 days, set expectations, and outline any next steps if you intend to have them build their own 60-90 plan.

- What training should be completed in the first 30 days?
- Is there anyone they should shadow?
- What does success for someone in their specific position look like 30 days from now?

#20

TEACH FAST

One of the keys to making the biggest impact on your employees is speed. When you teach quickly, you give your people the momentum they need to become unstoppable right away.

Telling you to teach fast is easy enough, but to teach fast, this principle needs to become a part of the company culture:

- Organize a team of company leaders who can help implement a "teaching fast" policy (curriculum, timelines, etc.), provide expertise from past experience, and deal with any pain points that come up along the way.
- Put together small, hands-on instructional workshops where employees can practice the skills needed for their role.
- As you implement "teach fast" strategy, collect case studies of employees who've achieved great success as a result to inspire other employees.

#21

INVEST IN TRAINING AND TECHNOLOGY FOR THE TEAM

The team can't succeed without the right training to master the job. The team can't succeed without the right tools and technologies to outperform at the job.

With this in mind, it's important to invest in both for your team and never forget that this investment doesn't end. You can always provide more training, tools, and technologies to help your team maximize its success.

You succeed only when your team succeeds.

Always invest in training and technology for the team.

#22

BUY YOURSELF LEVERAGE

Leverage is time, and the best way to buy yourself time is by hiring top people to get the job done. Any time you are doing something that takes a lot of time and work that you probably shouldn't be doing, it's time to buy yourself some leverage and hire experts on the team who can get the job done better, faster, and smarter!

Every quarter, I have to coach my team to hire the people they need to scale their leverage.

Many of the people on your team will want to do it all, control it all, manage it all, and not bring other people in. Coach your managers to continue hiring people who buy them leverage, which will create more time for them to do their best work.

#23

START A MENTORSHIP PROGRAM

Once every entry-level employee gets through the first 90 days, enter them into a mandatory year-long mentorship program. Choose senior-level rock stars to act as mentors, and be clear about the responsibilities and guiding principles the mentors should abide by.

To draw the greatest value from mentorships, mentors and mentees should meet on a regular basis and discuss the following:

- Top 1% habits.
- Obstacles mentors faced when they started out and what they did to overcome them.
- The steps they took to advance to their current position.

As a mentor, the goal is to share any and all secrets you wished you would have known when you started, from mindset to professionalism to very specific, position-related issues.

Lastly, just like everything in leadership, study the data and optimize, optimize, optimize. Survey your mentors and mentees (anonymously), and figure out ways you can make the program better. Work to make your mentorship program one of the top in your industry, because when new employees receive the guidance they need, retention rates go up.

#24

TEACH NEW TEAM MEMBERS TO STUDY TOP EMPLOYEES

Anytime you have a new team member, I recommend you have them shadow the best people on your team.

Here are some questions a new team member could ask and document for their development:

- How do they communicate with the team?
- How do they manage their execution plans?
- How do they structure their day to maximize productivity?
- How do they manage and prioritize their task list?
- How in-depth are their completed projects or pipeline?
- How do they manage their calendar?
- How do they respond to new requests?
- How do they brainstorm ideas, strategies, and solutions to problems?
- What would they have done differently in the first 30–90 days of starting the job?

#25

WHEN ONBOARDING, SHARE THE TOP 20% DATA

One key to successfully onboarding individual contributors is to share the performance data of your top performers. Create a list of the performance data and results they produce.

- Daily
- Weekly
- Monthly
- Quarterly
- Annually

Sharing what the top 20% are doing gives new employees targets to go after. This also ensures that every person on the team understands the most important numbers to track.

To share an example, let's say I hired a sales rep who would be responsible for booking appointments with prospects. To get them ramped up, I would share the following daily numbers that a top performer in that position hits:

- Number of sales calls
- Number of sales emails
- Number of social LinkedIn messages
- Number of meetings booked
- Number of meetings held
- Cold-to-booked click-through rate
- Number of closed won sales
- Average revenue

If people know what the best are doing in their position, they will ramp up faster, exceed goals, and make more money faster. Knowing these numbers will help a new employee do exactly that and crush it.

#26
DELIVER POSITIVE FEEDBACK FOR IMPROVEMENT

The greatest leaders that I've had the pleasure to work with always shared positive feedback for improvement using this simple formula:

Positive compliment + Biggest goal/desire/dream + Opportunity for improvement = Results generated from change

Here's how it breaks down:

- **Positive compliment:** Before you give constructive feedback, always start with something nice about the employee (their work ethic, their coachability, etc.). This softens the "blow" and makes them more receptive to your feedback.

- **Biggest goal/dream/desire:** Acknowledge the employee's major goals. This reminds them that you are in their corner, and (like the compliment) it helps them stay open-minded to your feedback.
- **Opportunity for improvement:** Frame your feedback as a chance to improve performance and increase results rather than a negative.

Here's an example of an opportunity for improvement:

> "Tina, one opportunity for improvement here is to use a multichannel approach. I noticed from the data in the CRM that 90% of your outbound sales activity is email, 8% is LinkedIn, and 2% is outbound calling. Why don't you start leveraging the phone more so you can book more appointments? In case you're not sure how to make the most out of calls, here's how I would approach a call. . . ."

With this example, instead of attacking Tina for not using all sales channels, we're framing the feedback as an educational opportunity and giving actionable tasks she can execute today.

- **Results that can be generated:** Tie everything back to the results that can be generated if the employee changes. For example, if you have a rep who is dying to buy a house, discuss how booking more qualified demos (the opportunity for improvement) will increase their income and help them get their dream house faster.

There you have it! This is the ultimate formula for delivering constructive feedback that makes your employees feel empowered to take their success in their own hands.

#27
HOLD EFFECTIVE ONE-ON-ONE MEETINGS: SKIP LEVEL TEMPLATE

This meeting template is a great starting point for senior managers or executives connecting with individuals they don't directly manage.

Company Strategy

Here are some conversation starters to pulse-check alignment on strategy and goals:

- What is something you are unclear about as it relates to the company's short- and long-term goals?
- What is something you think we should start or stop doing?

Career Development

Here are some conversation starters to pulse-check career development:

- What are your career goals in the next 6 to 12 months? How would you say you're progressing toward those goals?
- Are you happy in your current role? What would make things better?

#28

MAKE YOUR ONE-ON-ONE MEETINGS CROSS-FUNCTIONAL

This is a great template to use for general check-ins between members of different teams that have to regularly work together.

Team Collaboration

Figure out what is working and what is not with one-on-one meetings and across-team collaborations.

- How has the collaboration with our department been for you lately?
- What have been some recent wins and challenges between our teams?
- What can I do to make your job easier?

Planning and Priorities

Figure out the game plan between now and the next one-on-one meeting.

- Looking ahead, what are the biggest challenges on the horizon for you?
- What are your upcoming priorities and goals?
- What is one thing we could partner on that would accelerate both of our teams?

#29

DON'T TAKE EMPLOYEE CHURN TOO PERSONALLY

An employee who quits is not your enemy. Never forget that no business promises lifetime employment, just like no employee promises lifetime loyalty.

Before the team member leaves, do the following:

- Learn why they took a new position working for the other company.
- Learn what they loved about working for you and the company.
- Learn how you can improve with the next replacement.

Then leverage this data to make changes as you see fit.

#30

HIRE HIGHER

Hire people who you hope could take your job one day. If you want to build a world-class team, always try to "hire higher." The better others are, the better you are. The better the team is around you, the better you are.

Hire people who could take your job one day!

#31

DON'T FORGET THE NUMBER-ONE REASON PEOPLE JOIN STARTUPS

If you work for a startup, then this secret is tailor-made for you. I want you to know that there are a few reasons people join startups.

- Greater creative freedom.
- Greater tech innovation.
- Fast-paced career growth.
- Your opinion about the daily operations of the company actually matters.
- A casual work environment.
- You get to work with people who are doing whatever it takes to succeed, instead of people who are disenchanted with their work.

I could list even more reasons, but the number-one reason why people decide to join a startup is because you get to be a part of something bigger than yourself. You get the pleasure of waking up every morning and knowing that you and your team are working to change the world and to transform people's lives. Ultimately, getting to be a part of something greater than yourself creates a sense of fulfillment you won't get at many companies.

So if your organization is a startup, don't forget this, and remind your team of that greater mission every day.

MONTH 3

DEVELOPING A HIGH-PERFORMANCE CULTURE

#1

THE TEAM'S SUCCESS IS YOUR SUCCESS

I sign my email signature "Your Success Is My Success" because I fundamentally believe it. I like to coach my team, my customers, and my investors that regardless of their decision or outcome, their success is my success.

To become a great leader, you should teach your team to do the same and bring out the best in each other. Surround your team with people who push each other to do better.

No negativity. No drama. Just higher goals and higher motivation. Good times and positive energy. No jealousy. No hate.

Just simply working together every day to bring out the absolute best in each other.

#2

BUILD AN AMAZING CULTURE

As a leader, you don't build amazing culture by offering free snacks, ping-pong tables, open seating, or gym memberships.

You build amazing culture by talking to your team and working hard to understand what they care about. You build an amazing culture by talking to your people and listening intently to what they need to succeed.

Then work hard on delivering what people care about and what they need to succeed.

#3

LEARN THE FOUR KEYS TO A BALANCED WORK CULTURE

The companies that constantly dust the competition all have one thing in common: balance.

Work–life balance. Balance between hard work (and all the stress-induced growth the best work requires) and the euphoria of success.

You want to create a work culture where there's a healthy balance of positivity, challenge, accomplishment, and camaraderie. Between these four elements, if anything gets out of whack, the stress on your workers will skyrocket.

For example, if there is too much challenge without much positivity or if there's a great sense of team unity but no mission or objective that's challenging enough to inspire pride, your people won't be inclined to produce top-quality work.

If you can create an environment where all four of these elements are in perfect balance, your employees will be inspired to put in their best effort every single day.

#4

BRING OUT THE CREATIVE GENIUS IN YOUR TEAM

Your team loves to create new things that solve problems at your company. Unfortunately, many of us as leaders will try to push our own ideas and strategies onto the team. Sometimes this is good because you know the solution that's needed for your team to execute. Other times it blocks the team's creativity.

Work hard to unlock the creativity and problem-solving strategies of the team. Tell the team the goal or the problem, and give them the space to get creative, get their hands dirty, and work to solve it.

Unlock the creative genius inside the team and don't let your ego block the path.

#5

HELP SPREAD ROCK-STAR QUALITIES

While toxic behaviors can spread across a team quickly, amazing, rock-star behaviors can also make a similar impact.

As a manager, you want to do everything you can to spot those rock-star qualities. When I say rock-star qualities, I mean traits like adaptability, not a technical skill that requires training like coding.

Make sure that these rock-star qualities are behaviors that can be learned and picked up quickly. Then help spread the best rock-star qualities by taking these steps:

1. **Identify it:** During team meetings, point out people on your team who demonstrate a specific rock-star quality and the results they're producing. This encourages others to imitate this behavior.
2. **Increase collaboration:** During hectic situations, give people the chance to collaborate with the rock stars as much as possible so they can see how the stars respond in different situations, what they make a priority, and how they solve problems.
3. **Reward rock-star behavior:** Give public praise and rewards so there's an incentive for team members to adapt these qualities.

#6

TEACH YOUR TEAM TO GO THE EXTRA MILE

If you want to get ahead in a job, a career, or a business, go the extra mile. The person who does more than they're paid for will soon be paid for more than what they do.

Coach your team to never say the following:

"This isn't my job."

"I don't know how."

"I'm not paid to do this."

Or, "That's not part of my job description."

Every day we are all doing things that we were never trained or prepared to do, but when there's a will, there's a way.

The people who go the extra mile and find "the way" become the all-in leaders of tomorrow.

#7

DO THE HARD THINGS

Keep doing the hard things until the hard things become the easy things.

Progress > Perfection.

#8

THE SUM IS GREATER THAN THE PARTS

Coach your team that alone they can accomplish a little. However, together as a team, they can achieve 10 times what they can do alone.

#9

TRAINING NEVER STOPS

For successful people, the training never stops.

- You can always get better than where you are right now.
- You can always get smarter than who you are right now.
- You can always learn more than what you've learned right now.
- You can always improve.

Coach the team that the best never stop training on their journey to success.

#10

STUDY YOUR GAME FILM

Regardless of the sport, every great player studies game film. Game film is a recording of a game at various angles for the purposes of review. A player will analyze game film so they can study the plays that were a success and the plays that were a failure.

If you thought game film applied only to sports, you're wrong, because no matter what industry you're in, your employees can document their own game film.

Whether it's recordings of calls or meetings with customers, prospects, etc., have your team members send you their game film for feedback and performance improvement.

You can also have them submit it to be reviewed as part of a team coaching session. But encourage your team members to share their game film because it demonstrates a desire to want to improve. And it demonstrates how they are a cut above the rest.

#11
FIGURE OUT THE "ONE THING"

One of the biggest ways I helped my team improve their performance was going from trying to improve nine different areas of performance to focusing on one major area or "One Thing."

Imagine you have two people on a deserted island, and the only thing to eat is three rabbits. The person who tries to catch all three rabbits catches nothing. But the person who focuses on hunting one rabbit will succeed. They'll develop a hunting strategy and, most importantly, live to hunt another day.

The same analogy applies to coaching. The leader who coaches their employees to improve a ton of variables at once accomplishes nothing. But the leader who focuses on improving just one variable at a time succeeds.

For example, if I wanted to coach my sales team and apply this analogy, during one month I would focus on increasing their number of opportunities. I would coach them on building more prospecting lists, working more referrals to get more deals, and flooding the calendar with back-to-back appointments.

By focusing on one variable at a time, my team can see bigger results and even double their number of opportunities that month. When you try to get your team to improve too many variables at once, they get overwhelmed, and nothing changes for the better. But if you focus on one area at a time, your teams gets thorough coaching and the time to perfect their skills.

Now that you know the value of focusing on one variable at a time, my question to you is: what is the one thing your team could improve on that will help improve the trajectory of the company forever? Focus on that "One Thing" over the next month.

#12
ADD INSANE VALUE

Deliver so much value, training, support, coaching, education, tools, tech, data, processes, playbooks, and systems that your team doesn't need your advice anymore.

When you deliver value consistently and predictably, eventually it scales all on its own to the point that they won't need you any longer, which is what you want!

#13
ADOPT A BIAS TOWARD ACTION

Nobel Prize winner Rabindranath Tagore once said, "You can't cross the sea merely by standing and staring at the water."

You can't get where you want in your career and in your life without action. When you start taking action toward your goals, people with similar goals will align with you.

Things that once seemed confusing become clear. Your confidence grows. And you start to become more fully engaged in all areas of your life. For you to achieve more than you have before, develop a bias toward consistent action.

#14
YOUR NEXT VICTORY REQUIRES A SINGLE STEP

As you take action, you learn more at a faster rate than if you sit, wait, and think about a decision.

Many high achievers have said that their secret to success is to fail faster than anyone else, and the only way to fail and move on to your next great win is to take action.

Just do it! A journey of a thousand miles always begins with a single step.

#15
ALWAYS ASK "WHY?"

Never be content with the way things are at your company. Always stay curious about everything, and get into the habit of asking questions like these:

- Why does it take X amount of time to perform Y task?
- Why is this tool in our tech stack?
- Why is this a priority?
- Why is this the way we measure success?

Constantly ask yourself "why?" because "why?" always leads to better solutions.

#16

MEASURE YOUR SUCCESS BY HOW MANY PEOPLE THANK YOU FOR THEIRS

Success = Your impact on others.

Happiness = Your gratitude for how far you've come with impacting others.

Always strive to help your team maximize their success every day, and you will make an impact.

When you succeed, there is only one story to tell. When you help others succeed, there are 100 stories to tell and 1,000 stories to inspire.

Give more and you will always get more in return, never less.

#17

CREATE A SCALABLE, REPEATABLE, AND PREDICTABLE PLAYBOOK FOR YOUR TEAM

Create a predictable, repeatable, scalable process for all the conversations you're going to have. And treat your playbooks like frequently asked questions (FAQs) or scripts.

- For instance, if a sales prospect says, "I want to cancel," what should your reps say?
- If a job candidate says, "They're happy where they're at," how should your recruiters respond?

- If a client wants to know why they can't get access to a certain feature, how should your customer success reps react?

Think of yourself as a coach. You need the playbook to maximize your success in business and life.

As a manager, you need to have the most robust playbook, so always optimize your playbook for you and your team. This will help you create the highest- performing business model for your department.

#18
BECOME AN EXPERT IN YOUR FIELD

One of your goals in your journey to becoming an all-in leader is to become an expert in your field.

The best of the best in every industry have so much knowledge from experience and studying, they practically have a PhD in their field. If you want to become an expert in your industry, you need to have an insatiable hunger to learn and a natural curiosity that makes you question everything about your industry.

Constantly asking questions and doing the research to find the answers is the foundation of expert knowledge. Set up interviews with mentors, learn from your experiences, and take ownership of your education.

If you carry out these actions consistently over a period of time, you'll become a world-class expert in your industry in no time.

#19

SENIORITY DOESN'T MEAN ANYTHING

People think that because they have seniority, they are owed something. Could you imagine if LeBron James showed up to a game and said, "I'm not going to play today because last year I won the national championship."? LeBron James would get traded in two seconds flat.

Too many people think that seniority means they can be lazy, but seniority doesn't mean that. What you did yesterday is irrelevant. The only thing that matters is what you do today.

Don't rely on seniority to demand respect and money because you're only as hot as your last win.

#20

BE OBSESSED WITH MAXIMIZING THE PERFORMANCE OF YOUR TEAM

In any management position, you always want to think, how can I help the team improve?

My advice is to look at the data, find opportunities for improvement, and obsess over the training.

Does your team have a lot of activity but no booked appointments? Then there's a messaging issue.

Do they have booked appointments but no activity? Then there's a motivation issue.

Low activity? They don't know what to say or how to say it. Focus on training them and boosting their confidence so they're not afraid to do the activity.

If it's a book-to-held issue, that means the rep is not getting the commitment to close right when they have the prospect on the line.

If it's a held-closed-won-deal problem in the funnel, then maybe they're not targeting the right people.

Some of these scenarios apply specifically to sales just for the sake of sharing an example, but regardless of your industry, take this as an illustration of what you want to do for your team: identify the pain point, locate the root cause, and develop a plan to fix it.

Every day when you wake up as a leader, you need to run through the issues your team is having and focus on what you can do to help them win today.

#21
SURVEY YOUR TEAM ON YOUR MANAGEMENT

The best way to monitor the development of your future leaders is to train them, coach them, track the data, and survey the impact of their hard work on their people. This means that surveying and collecting feedback from your people on the experience of their leaders is absolutely critical to continue to improve results.

Here are some management evaluation questions you can ask your team to answer:

- Does your manager give you concrete feedback that you can execute?
- Does your manager give you the space needed to complete tasks to the best of your ability?

- Does your manager seem to care about your personal life (mental health, personal goals, etc.)?
- Does your manager do a good job of managing deadlines/priorities and so on?
- Is your manager invested in your career development?
- Is your manager clear about expectations?
- What would you recommend your manager change or improve?

I recommend tailoring these survey questions for your team and organization and checking in with your team regularly.

At Seamless.AI, we collect feedback on our leaders two to four times a year. No one will ever be perfect; however, we should always strive for perfection.

#22
BOOST PRODUCTIVITY BY ELIMINATING BOTTLENECKS

To empower your team to complete projects in a timely manner, here are some productivity red flags that make efficiency impossible:

- **There's a clear problem that no one is taking responsibility for:** A lot of times this is an issue that the company is aware of because it slows down internal processes, but instead of eliminating the problem, everyone just accepts it.
- **The problem doesn't have a paper trail:** Often with bottleneck issues, everyone comes up with their own unique way of working around the problem, and the costs of that extra time and labor are never calculated. This is a telltale sign of a productivity issue because no one knows how much the issue is costing them month to month.

The greatest leaders identify these problems and work to eliminate them without being asked to do so. And because these types of leaders refuse to accept that it's just "the way things are," their team can be more productive and the company benefits overall.

#23

REWARD EMPLOYEES FOR THEIR IDEAS TO IMPROVE

Work to reward employees for sharing their ideas, advice, thoughts, and recommendations to improve the team.

- Ideas to improve results
- Ideas to improve speed to market
- Ideas to improve communication
- Ideas to improve culture
- Ideas to improve recruiting

Employees love getting recognized and rewarded for their ideas.

Create a way to track and reward employees who are constantly helping you and the team become the best that you can be. This reward can be in the form of paid time off, bonuses, commissions, prize money, trips—you name it.

#24

PLACE PEOPLE WHERE THEY ARE A PERFECT FIT

So you hire a new person for your team knowing that they will be a great fit. They start out strong, but by the end of the first month, it's clear they aren't thriving at their job. The next step is to let them go as quickly as possible, right?

Wrong.

Unless this person ends up being toxic to the team, the last thing you want to do is give your competitors the advantage by letting good talent go. Instead of firing them, move them to another position that speaks to their interests.

You're going to change their life by introducing them to a career they're passionate about, and your company can continue to benefit from their abilities.

#25
GIVE YOUR PEOPLE FREEDOM AND CREATIVE SPACE

Always give your people the freedom to try new strategies, new software—you name it!

Give your people permission to revise internal processes and experiment with new ways of finishing tasks.

You want to create a space where risks can be taken without repercussion because big risks mean big wins, smashing records, and raising the bar. What causes a lot of teams to plateau is allowing only leaders to take risks and execute ideas.

Instead of enforcing a hierarchy where decisions come only from the top down, create a space where everyone is free to share their ideas even if they seem "crazy."

#26

BE YOUR TEAM'S BIGGEST CHEERLEADER

When your team wins, you should always be the biggest cheerleader. Be hyped! Let your team know how proud you are of them.

You want to give a lot of public praise because it's one of the greatest ways to boost morale. When you regularly give shout-outs, it motivates your people to continue working hard because they'll keep striving for that praise.

Giving public praise also boosts camaraderie. When you're cheering on your team's accomplishments, your employees will follow your lead and celebrate each other's wins.

Make a point to carve out time during meetings to give shout-outs for the big and small wins that your team scores for the company.

#27

GIVE ALL THE CREDIT WHEN YOU WIN, TAKE ALL THE BLAME WHEN YOU LOSE

The next time your team has a major win, give them all the credit. Take zero ownership and shine the spotlight on your team.

While giving credit wins people over and builds relationships, taking responsibility when things go wrong is what earns trust.

So many employees have anxiety about making mistakes because they're afraid of all the possible ramifications. They could get a strike or, worse, lose their job. To avoid this, make it a point to take ownership when failure happens.

It will alleviate the pressure on your people's backs and motivate them to take chances because they will know that if the risk doesn't work out, you will have their back.

#28

HELP YOUR TEAM MAKE FRIENDS AT WORK

There are studies that show if your people have friends at work, they're much more likely to stay and grow with the company. With this in mind, coach your people on how to develop great meaningful relationships at work.

Help your people realize that working together to maximize each other's success will only help each other grow. The more friends your co-workers have at work, the happier they will be. Help them make meaningful relationships, and you will have a successful team culture.

#29

NO MATTER THE JOB, ACKNOWLEDGE HOW HARD YOUR PEOPLE WORK

No job is easy. Your team and every individual contributor who works for you will spend more time on the job than with their friends and family. In fact, we all spend at least 265 days out of the year at work.

This is why it is critical to celebrate all the wins, both big and small. You want to help the team stay engaged, excited, inspired, and dedicated to serving the mission and the customers you are trying to impact.

All wins are exciting, so be sure to celebrate them for all your people.

#30

POSITIVE REINFORCEMENT TRUMPS NEGATIVE REINFORCEMENT

To generate long-term behavior change, utilize positive reinforcement over negative reinforcement. Recognize and congratulate your team constantly for the actions, behaviors, cultural attributes, and results they support at work.

There are team members who you probably haven't thanked or supported in weeks. Change that and thank them for their hard work today. Make sure you leverage positive recognition with the team as much as possible.

#31

CREATE A CULTURE OF CONTINUOUS LEARNING AND DEVELOPMENT

If you want to build the best team, you have to invest the best in the team.

At our company, every team trains for at least 30 minutes a day. We have live coaching calls, training sessions, etc. because one of the greatest leadership mistakes that hurt growth is a lack of professional development.

To avoid this, create a recurring and diverse training calendar that is repeatable, scalable, and predictable for your team to constantly develop and improve.

PART II

THE STRATEGIES FOR BUILDING
HIGH-PERFORMING TEAMS

MONTH 4

KPIs, GOAL SETTING, AND DECISION-MAKING

#1

FIND YOUR DAILY DOSE
OF INSPIRATION IN YOUR "WHY"

If you're ready to start getting up every day motivated to tackle your goals, the key is being clear on what your "why" is. Your "why" is your personal mission statement. It's the root reason for all of your actions.

Understanding your "why" is so important because it's like a fly-wheel. Once you know your "why," the goals you need to create and the daily actions you need to take all become crystal clear.

Knowing your "why" makes everything in life fall into place. When you know your "why," you don't need to spend a fortune on motivational coaches and training courses because you've unlocked your core purpose. When you do this, the passion and the focus become second nature.

When you work every day to get one step closer to that core purpose, you'll be so much happier, and the positivity will spread and impact everyone around you.

Knowing your "why" isn't beneficial just for you; it's also great for your team because it builds direction and camaraderie.

To make finding your "why" easier, the first thing you and your team should do is reflect on your lives and careers thus far.

- What have been your greatest accomplishments?
- What moments are you the proudest of?

The reason I ask you to identify your successes is because these are the moments where you were operating at the top of your game.

These are the moments when your passion was at its highest. And this is all key to figuring out your "why."

So, identify these moments and look for similarities and patterns that keep coming up.

- What were you doing that led to this success?
- Were you helping someone?
- Were you identifying a solution to a problem?

Once you and your team know your "why," you can unlock your maximum potential and tap into an endless source of passion and happiness.

#2

EVALUATE YOUR JUDGMENT

When you hear the word *leader*, discernment is probably one of the last skills that comes to mind, but it's crucial to becoming a world-class manager.

Depending on how big your company is, more times than not, as a manager, you'll be given a goal with little to no guidance or explanation. In these situations, you need to have discernment to fill in the gaps and make sense of the abstract for your team. If you have no idea where to begin with honing your discernment skills, start sharpening your judgment in areas you are already strong in.

I suggest this because areas where you naturally crush it will also be areas where you have tons of intuitive ability. This intuitive ability lends itself to discernment. For example, if data analysis is a natural strength, hone your discernment here and predict industry trends or opportunities for expansion that your team can take advantage of.

To problem solve with maximum efficiency, work on your ability to discern.

#3

LEADERS ARE READERS

At the age of 25, I turned a new page and found an incredible secret that helped me catapult from average results to unstoppable success.

Prior to unlocking this secret, I tried to build different companies. Many were failures until I unlocked one of the secrets that changed everything...reading!

That's right, reading was fundamental to my success because books have cheat codes for everything you need in life. I've read hundreds of books. And to this day, on average, I spend one to two hours a day reading expert advice.

If you want a better life, but you don't read, my advice to you is this: success is a muscle, and books help strengthen it. So take the time to read because you can quite literally read and study your way out of the lowest points in life.

One of the tricks here is to read books that help you solve the problems you face today or the opportunities you are looking to capitalize on tomorrow.

1. Identify a problem you want to solve or an opportunity you are eager to seize.
2. Find the top three to five books on the topic. Leverage best-seller rankings, reviews on Amazon, etc. to make your choice.
3. Read at least 5–10 pages a day.
4. Execute the action plan and put in the work to make it happen.

#4

TRAIN YOUR TEAM TO BE THE BEST PLAYERS

A manager who trains their people to be the best team players they can possibly be is great. But someone who trains their employees to be leaders themselves is the best of the best.

In other words, don't just train your employees to do their job well. Train them to be independent thinkers and problem solvers. If an issue comes up and your people have no idea what to do until you get involved, that's costing the company money and time it can't get back.

But if your employees can come up with solutions on their own, your organization can run like a well-oiled machine.

There are countless ways you can train and mentor your employees to be leaders. Instead of always focusing on the daily grind, get your people to think bigger.

During team meetings and one-on-ones, be transparent about the organization's annual goals, and have your employees discuss how their projects and daily tasks connect to these larger company goals.

Give stretch assignments where you're tasking an employee with a project that requires them to go beyond their skill set. This will challenge employees to work through problem areas, grow under pressure, and perform at the level of a leader.

#5

SHOW INTEGRITY 24/7 (EVEN WHEN NO ONE IS WATCHING)

If you want to become an all-in leader, you need to make it your goal to instill integrity in your team. But what exactly is integrity?

Integrity includes always doing the right thing, but when it comes to leadership, integrity also includes the following:

- Honesty
- Reliability
- Selflessness
- Accountability

Integrity doesn't mean doing the right thing only when you have an audience. True integrity means possessing these qualities at all times, even when no one is watching.

You want to always be a pillar of integrity for your team to model so that when they have to make decisions on their own, they know what to do and how to conduct themselves to represent the company in the best light.

#6

GETTING THINGS WRONG IS AN INTEGRAL PART OF GETTING THINGS RIGHT

Many teams invest a lot of time and money into making a decision only to later realize it may not have been the right one. Then these leaders decide to keep pressing ahead because they aren't humble enough to change their mind when they need to do so.

With this secret, I want to tell you that it's OK for you and the team to change your minds! In fact, you have permission to change your mind whenever you need to do so.

Just because you decide on a direction doesn't mean you have to commit to that path forever. And you don't want to continue executing a flawed plan that takes your team in the wrong direction because you're afraid of a bruised ego.

Growth is found only in change. And getting things wrong is a part of getting things right.

#7

FAVOR RESULTS OVER TIME

Manage your team based on the results they generate, not the amount of time they spend chained to their desk. If you have someone who is always online from 8 a.m. to 6 p.m. but not producing any results versus someone who is absolutely crushing their results in fewer hours, who would you prefer as an employee?

As an all-in leader, you want to focus on managing your team for results, not hours they've clocked in.

Make sure that all your evaluations track outcomes and deliverables instead of hours clocked in because it's all about results over time.

#8

DON'T SWEAT THE SMALL STUFF

Overthinking a decision slows down action, progress, and overall growth. When mistakes happen, always act quickly on things that are easy to change. And act slowly on the things that are irreversible and hard to change.

The faster you can help your team make decisions and avoid overthinking, the better.

#9

CREATE KEY PERFORMANCE INDICATORS

To keep your employees focused on growing the organization, they need to create their own key performance indicators (KPIs).

KPIs are job-related goals that align with the larger mission of the company. It could be a project, an ad campaign, or a certain number of closed deals, but a KPI is a specific goal—broken down into smaller monthly, quarterly, and annual goals—that you and the employee can track their progress on.

One of the many benefits of KPIs is that they help you objectively evaluate your employees. With KPIs, it isn't a mystery to the employee what you expect from them. KPIs will show them where there's room for improvement without you having to be the villain.

#10
IDENTIFY YOUR TEAM'S GOALS

It is difficult to inspire team members to accomplish tasks without understanding their biggest problems and their greatest goals.

When you understand what motivates your employees, you can help them realize that the work they do every day is getting them closer to the dreams that matter the most to them.

Meet with each of your team members and have them list their four pillars of goals.

Four Goal Pillars

- Professional goals
- Personal goals
- Health goals
- Miscellaneous goals

Then have each team member share what their goals are for these pillars and help them create an action plan.

Not only does this exercise help each team member accomplish their goals as efficiently as possible, but imagine how great your teammate feels when they have a manager who truly cares about them? That's when the magic happens and your team's potential gets unleashed!

#11
SET AQMD GOALS

AQMD is a helpful acronym that represents every kind of goal your employees should work toward. AQMD stands for Annual, Quarterly, Monthly, and Daily. Everything your employees do, from their daily workflow to priorities, should revolve around their AQMD goals.

AQMD will help you identify your employees' top KPIs and break them down into measurable daily, monthly, quarterly, and annual goals.

This acronym is a perfect example of compounding interest and how daily work turns into weekly, monthly, quarterly, and annual wins.

To show you the power of compounding interest, let's say, for example, that my sales target for the year is $1,000,000 and there are 265 sales days in a year (excluding weekends, holidays, PTO, etc.). This means that if I had one salesperson on my team responsible for $1,000,000, I would take $1,000,000 and divide that number by 265.

This would give me the daily sales goal needed to hit my $1,000,000 annual target: $3,774. So for my salesperson to generate more than $1,000,000 per year, they would need to sell $3,774 per day.

Whatever department you are in, quantifiably define the annual goals of your employees and team members. Break them down in the following table and walk your team members through them:

- Annual goals
  (X)
- Quarterly goals
  (Y) = X / 4
- Monthly goals
  (Z) = X / 12
- Daily goals
  (Q) = X / 265

For the $1,000,000 example:

- Annual Goal:
  $1,000,000
- Quarterly Goal:
  $250,000
- Monthly Goal:
  $83,334
- Daily Goal:
  $3,774

It doesn't matter whether you are in sales, marketing, finance, etc., to get ahead of your biggest dreams, you have to break them down AQMD-style.

#12
TACKLE THE BIG PICTURE WITH QUARTERLY REVIEWS

Quarterly reviews are one-on-one meetings where you and your employee examine their wins and "stuck-ons" over the past quarter.

During quarterly reviews, take a look at the following:

- Data (KPI and performance data)
- Work completed
- Playbooks
- Processes
- Systems
- Goals

With quarterly reviews, let the employee lead the conversation and give them the space to reflect on the following:

- What went well the past three months?
- What could be improved from the past three months?
- What are the next steps to make the next quarter bigger than the last?

As a reminder, if your employee didn't end up meeting their goals, quarterly review meetings are not the time to be negative.

Instead of criticizing, now is the time to listen and think about new habits and more precise goals for the employee to execute over the next quarter.

- What actions, strategies, etc. didn't work out this quarter that you should stop doing for the next quarter?
- What can I, as your manager, do to help you win more?

In addition to KPIs and annual goals, another big topic you will want to tackle during quarterly reviews is where the employee is at in their career development.

- Over the next quarter, what skills and experience would you like to pick up to get better at your job?
- Where is your progress on your annual goals (are you crushing it? Are things slow?)?

Taking the time to discuss career development separates all-in leaders from mere managers because it forces you and your employee to think bigger here. You want your employee to go beyond the grind of day-to-day tasks and to think instead about what they can do to maximize their raw potential.

Taking this approach to quarterly reviews is only going to help you learn more about your people and the growth they want to get out of their jobs. Be sure to draft a summary of meeting key points and share them with your employees once you wrap up all your quarterly reviews.

#13
COACH YOUR TEAM TO PROVIDE WEEKLY UPDATES

I learned this secret when I was fundraising nearly $100 million for my tech company, Seamless.AI. After my first round of funding, I realized that my investors kept asking for updates on the business every month, so I decided to create a monthly investor newsletter to give them everything they need. This newsletter worked so well with keeping everyone on the same page with goal progress that I realized this same type of content would be great for employees to regularly give to their leaders.

Coach your team to send you or anyone they indirectly report to a weekly update on what they are working on. If they can do this without fail every week, it will keep everyone aligned on what is getting done, as well as blockers along the way.

Here is the format I recommend:

Data: What is the latest data on the KPIs this person is working to improve?

What went well: What got done last week and what went well? Brag about the kick-ass stuff you got done.

Opportunities for improvement: What can be improved on from last week? It's OK for your employees to be vulnerable and share failures because this is how they improve.

Next steps: What are your top priorities over the next week?

Blockers /help needed: What do you need help with to complete? Is there anything or anyone blocking or holding up your success that your leader can help with?

Ideally, if you can get this automatically built into your systems, like Slack or KPI management software, to be completed every week, that will help maintain consistency of completion.

Additionally, by having this in an email format and in the management software, when you go back to do performance reviews, you can easily see everything that has been accomplished for every team member.

Educating your team on the importance of communicating their work and what is getting done ensures that everyone on the team is moving in the right direction.

#14

THERE ARE ONLY TWO OUTCOMES TO A DECISION

The decisions your people make today impact their future.

Every decision you make is either:

- An investment that gets you closer to success
- A loss that pushes you one step back from success.

Make the decisions today that your future self will thank you for.

#15

USE TEAM RECOMMENDATIONS TO MAKE THE RIGHT DECISIONS

Before you make a decision, find the most forthright people who have no problem disagreeing with you when you're wrong. Bounce your ideas off them and use this conversation to make your final decision.

The reason I suggest this is because the biggest threat to good decision-making is emotions. When you're stressed or anxious, these emotions can cloud your judgment and cause you to make poor decisions. Instead of acting on emotions, take the time to gather information and learn. Then converse with others and get their point of view before making a decision.

Remember that when you talk with others, don't enter the conversation wedded to your decision. Instead, realize that what you've come up with may not be the best, and there may be a better decision out there.

When you're responsible for a decision, make the best possible choice by eliminating emotions, doing your research, and consulting with others.

#16

RECOMMIT TO YOUR DECISIONS DAILY

A lot of us assume that management is all about being shrewd: taking in the facts, making clear-cut decisions, and moving on. But an amazing manager doesn't just make decisions and move on.

They stick around and make sure their decisions lead to successful results. Let's say I decide to be healthier, lose a couple of pounds, and gain some muscle.

It's one thing to make this my goal. But if I'm not sticking to it day in and day out, eating right and hitting the gym, I'm going to fail and wind up back at square one.

Be decisive about the moves you make, but take the time to check in on the progress to ensure that your projects have the greatest shot at success. This extra effort is what makes some managers the greatest leaders in the world.

#17

MULTITASKING IS DOING MORE BUT GETTING LESS

Multitasking is the golden rule that most people live by today, and we even associate productivity with your ability to handle multiple tasks at the same time. I think this approach is ridiculous, and it's actually counterintuitive to effective leadership. Unless you're a super-human, it's virtually impossible to complete multiple objectives well.

Think about it: if you work on 100 different things, this doesn't mean you're being productive and efficient. All this means is that you're doing a mediocre job at those 100 different tasks.

Instead, do a fantastic job at completing that one task or project well, and the results you generate will be 10x greater than the average results you would get from completing 100 tasks or projects. If you want to become a great leader and fully realize your potential, avoid multitasking and spreading yourself thin, and instead work on your concentration.

Figure out your priorities and focus on completing one priority at a time to the best of your ability.

#18
GOOD IS THE ENEMY OF GREAT

Where you are now as a team is the sum of the decisions you've made as the leader and the actions you've taken. If the team's performance isn't where you want it to be, your mindset needs to change. Stop tolerating mediocrity, and expect nothing short of greatness.

The amount of success you create, the money you make, and the results you drive all depend on your tolerance. If you tolerate mediocrity, you don't improve your circumstances. But if you only tolerate greatness, you empower your team to elevate themselves and your company.

Good is the enemy of great. Tolerate nothing less than greatness.

#19
AVOID DRAMA

Here's a management tip when an employee on your team tries to ask about ongoing drama.

Your best bet to avoid making a messy situation worse is to just remind them that their focus should be on their KPIs. Participating in any kind of drama would only be a distraction from the goals that could help them transform their career and their life forever and for the better.

Stay focused on your job and how you can become the best that you can be.

Nothing else matters.

#20
REVIEW YOUR DATA DAILY

Review your performance data daily. Compare today's performance to yesterday's. Compare this month's performance to last month's. Compare this quarter's performance to last quarter's.

What is going well, and what could be improved?

For any KPI areas that are going great, work with the team to identify how you can repeat those great results in other areas and departments. For any areas that are trending down, brainstorm with your people to improve results. Also, don't be scared to review the data openly with your team.

I post daily data performance reviews to the entire company on Slack, and I review the data with my leaders every week because you can't figure out what you did well and what needs improvement without reviewing the data and taking action.

#21
NEW DATA = NEW DECISIONS

Every day you will get new data that will give you more information about the decisions that you and the team made. If you execute a strategy and the resulting data is strong, keep going. If you execute a strategy and the data is signaling a bad decision, change course ASAP.

And just because you change course doesn't mean that your original decision was right or wrong. Honestly, there's no such thing as a right or wrong decision—just changes that either get you closer to your goal or further from it.

It's also OK to admit that a decision didn't bring the team closer to the goal as you initially anticipated. Managers who can admit that an idea or test failed are all-in leaders others will admire. So don't be scared to change strategy based on new information.

New data = New decisions.

#22
MAKE WORK FUN

Make work more fun for your employees and inject some friendly competition into the mix by creating a scoreboard that keeps track of your people's wins.

If you're in sales, keep a scoreboard of deals each sales rep is closing. Or if you're in recruiting, keep a scoreboard of new employees that each team member is signing on. Whatever industry you're in, keep a running scoreboard of a key metric, and make sure it is easily accessible for the team.

Creating a scoreboard is a great tactical move because instead of looking at work as something that your employees have to do, a scoreboard gives them direction as they work toward earning bragging rights for the month.

Friendly competition like this creates camaraderie, where your team is hyping each other up and encouraging each other to go harder and beat the winning number from the previous month.

#23
PUT YOUR MONEY WHERE YOUR MOUTH IS

As a manager, if all you do is give your people a pat on the back when they meet a goal, it won't take long for these gestures to start losing their magic. In fact, continuously giving public praise for stellar work without any concrete rewards means nothing. After a while, your people will start to resent the praise or, worse, feel exploited.

To avoid this, when your employees accomplish big things, put your money where your mouth is and give any of the following:

- Spot bonuses
- Trips
- Lunches/dinners with leadership
- Promotions
- Raises

Taking care of your people earns their trust.

If you're on the fence about being more generous with bonuses and raises, remember this: what's going to cost your organization the most isn't overpaying the hard-working employees; it's overpaying the mediocre employees. When you're overpaying employees who want to skate by, you're getting returns that are nowhere near equal to the money you're shoveling out. But when you give incentives to hard-working employees, they're only going to be inspired to do more.

Put your money where your mouth is and reward your rock stars.

#24
TEACH YOUR TEAM TO SPEAK UP

The squeaky wheel always gets the oil. Great leaders teach their teams to speak up for what they want.

There's a big misconception that to be a "great teammate," you've got to sit back and quietly accept whatever comes your way. Educate your team that this is a major false misconception.

Whether it's your professional or personal life goals, you have to take control. Teach your team to share what they want in business and in life. Teach the people you lead to never sleep on their dreams and to always speak up and ask for what they want.

If you want to get a promotion, speak up. If you want to switch departments or teams, speak up. Because if a leader doesn't know what their people want, they'll never be able to help them achieve their greatest dreams.

#25

LET YOUR TEAM DO THE PROBLEM-SOLVING

When it comes to problem-solving, bad managers fluctuate between two extremes. Either they're trying to figure out the problem by themselves so they can be right once again or, if they pass the problem on to their team, they're on everyone's back micromanaging them every step of the way. Nothing good comes from either mindset.

On the one hand, when you handle all the problem-solving, you're keeping your people from learning valuable lessons in decision-making. On the other hand, when you try to micromanage everyone, you're giving your people a license to be lazy. Whenever you micromanage, people lose their agency. Instead of figuring things out on their own, they sit around and wait for you to tell them what to do.

When problems come up, challenge your team to come up with a solution. You can do this by:

- Giving a minimum of information—just what your people will need to get started
- Working with your team to create an execution strategy

Your team should then lead the effort every step of the way, from the execution strategy to implementation. As the manager, your only job here is to provide encouragement.

Be your team's greatest cheerleader and remind them that they can do anything and everything with hard work and a positive mindset.

#26

TRUST YOUR PEOPLE AND EMPOWER THEM TO MAKE AN IMPACT

Too many leaders believe that "trust is earned." As a result, they don't trust their employees and they let their egos get in the way, which only leads to micromanagement.

The problem with this strategy is that it makes your team move slower in a world where speed is the key to survival. Simply put, empowering your people to be proactive is the only way to scale fast.

There's no way to know what someone is capable of without giving them a chance. Empower your people to make things happen. Trust your people to serve your mission and your customers!

#27

DON'T STRIP YOUR PEOPLE OF THEIR DECISION-MAKING POWERS

Instead of hiring "yes" people who are going to agree with every good and bad idea you have, hire people who are so dedicated to the success of the company that they don't have a problem with telling you the truth, even if it's critical or contradictory to what you want.

Hire people who tell you what they believe is the right decision, idea, or recommendation to accomplish the goals or solve the problems at hand.

#28

SPEED TO DECISION IS A COMPETITIVE ADVANTAGE FOR YOUR TEAM

To build a unicorn company and a team that changes the world, the speed of your decision-making is crucial. When your team makes fast decisions, they can execute more, learn more, and eventually win more.

#29

GREAT LEADERS DO WHATEVER IT TAKES TO IMPROVE THE PERFORMANCE OF THEIR TEAM MEMBERS

If I have to make a cold call, help a team member write a script, analyze sales calls, or negotiate contracts for a team member, I'm willing to do it all to make sure my team wins.

Great leaders will review an employee's KPI data and then drill in strategically and tactically with that employee. It doesn't matter if the task is big or small, hard or easy, fun or not fun. Great leaders do whatever it takes to help their employees improve.

#30
SUCCESS LEAVES SECRETS

No matter what you and your team want to accomplish, I can promise you there's someone out there who's been where you want to be and has written about their journey.

Teach this to your team and remind them that success leaves clues. Whatever goal your team is trying to crush, find out who the most successful people are and study everything about them (books, courses, blogs, masterminds, etc.). These people have the secrets to success. And not only do they know how to get to where you want to be, but they've made all the mistakes so that you can avoid them.

I personally spend a fortune on personal development (books, courses, masterminds, etc.) and meetings with experts that cut my learning curve in half.

Never forget that success leaves clues. Always seek to find the secrets to anything you want to achieve, and you will live a life of abundance.

MONTH 5

PRIORITIZING TASKS, DIAGNOSING ISSUES, AND TAKING ACTION

#1
IT'S EITHER A "HELL YES" OR A "HELL NO"

I'm on a mission to hire 1,000 new employees at Seamless.AI. It's a big goal, but my VP of marketing, Jonathan, told me that if I want to achieve it, I have to remember that with candidates, "It's either a hell yes or a hell no."

In other words, if you're interviewing candidates, you can only dedicate your time to those who are passionate about your organization. If they aren't passionate about your product, your mission, and your company culture—if they aren't saying "hell yes,"—then it's a "hell no."

If they aren't excited to work with you, then they're going to tell you "no" either now or later—pick your poison.

If you live by this principle, you will save yourself a lot of heartache and wasted time, and you'll surround yourself only with people who are just as dedicated to your organization as you are.

#2
SHARE THE COMPANY'S PRIORITIES WITH YOUR TEAM

To become the best team, everyone has to do whatever it takes to keep moving the goal post forward. Everyone must be willing to go above and beyond their role to crush it every single month.

For your people to be able to do this, as a manager, you have to make sure they're clear on what the biggest priorities are at the organization. This means you have to be radically transparent with your team.

Discuss new strategies and approaches the company wants to implement. Share what the company's goals are for the year and how the team's efforts fit into these larger goals. And share the overall progress toward these objectives.

Is the organization ahead of meeting the goals? Behind? On track? What can your team do to help with the pacing of these objectives?

You want to be radically transparent with your team because this lets them know what the priorities are and the work they should be doing to contribute to those priorities.

#3

MAP OUT THE BEST PATH FOR YOUR DESTINATION POINT

Anyone can pick a destination point they would like to get to. But a leader who goes all-in has the skills to map out the journey to get to that destination point.

Before the team even begins their journey, the best managers do their research and find out what it takes to increase the odds of success. Before you select a destination point and start steering your team to success, follow these steps:

- **Do your homework:** Before you start a journey, always do your homework. Figure out the costs for a project. I'm not just talking about financial cost, but the costs of time, effort, resources. . .you name it. Weigh the costs against the results to see if the journey is worth taking.
- **Seek out other opinions:** No matter how amazing the best leaders are, they accept that they don't know everything, and they take as much advice as they can get. You need to do the same and seek out advice before you start on a project.

- **Learn from the past:** A lot of managers are proactive. Instead of dwelling on the past, they're forward-thinking. Keep in mind I'm not telling you to obsess over the past, but if you want to take your game to the next level, it's crucial to get those valuable learning lessons from past wins and losses. Reflecting, learning, and optimizing sets amazing leaders apart from the rest.
- **Get started on your journey:** Once you weigh the costs versus the results, listen to the experts, and reflect on past experiences, get ready to head out on your journey with a positive outlook. You're going to crush it!

#4
EVERY FIRST WEEK OF THE MONTH, CLEAN UP YOUR PIPELINE

At the beginning of every new month, work with your team to clean up the pipeline.

Remove any tasks, projects, or opportunities that don't have any importance anymore. Kill all deals that keep getting pushed out or are never really going to close. Keep your pipeline of work super tight with the most important deals, projects, and tasks at the forefront.

Pipeline Cleanup Tasks

- Clean up your pipeline of projects.
- Clean up your pipeline of tasks.
- Clean up your pipeline of deals.

When you make it a priority to clean out your pipeline at the beginning of every month, you make a fresh slate and set yourself up for the greatest success.

#5
DIRECTION > SPEED

Everyone on a team worries about the speed and efficiency of their workflow.

- How fast can I get this done?
- How fast can I learn this?
- How fast can I get promoted?
- How fast can I beat my peers?
- How fast can we hit our goal?
- How fast can I complete this project?

Mentor the team to stop worrying about speed and start worrying more about direction. It's always better to move slowly in the right direction than fast in the wrong one.

#6
TEACH YOUR TEAM TO DO
THE THINGS THEY NEED TO DO

Ask your team to write down what comes to mind when you say this out loud:

"You know what to do, you're just not doing it."

It can be anything.

- Reading more
- Having tough conversations with co-workers
- Increasing activity
- Removing toxic friends

Ask this question every week, and help your team get these tasks completed so they can level up.

#7

MAKE YOUR TEAM
A MERITOCRACY

One of the most common complaints employees have about their company is the bureaucracy. Everyone hates the paper trail that organizations make them go through to do every little thing.

While organizations put up a lot of safety guards to ensure that the best decisions are made, bureaucracy slows down internal processes. If you have the power to cut down on bureaucracy, I urge you to do less rather than more.

- **Simplify decision-making processes:** Keep your decision-makers down to the necessary few.
- **Cut down on redundant paperwork:** Make sure you don't have paperwork that requests the same info.
- **Cut down on meetings:** Meet only if it's the easiest way to communicate with the least amount of back-and-forth messaging.
- **Focus on the end goal:** Instead of focusing on the approval process that makes your organization no money, focus on the potential results.
- **Give your people greater reins to make decisions:** Train your people so that they are equipped to make decisions with less red tape.
- **Encourage decision-makers to act now:** There's always one decision-maker who will let a form sit on their desk for weeks. Remind every decision-maker of the urgency of the situation and encourage them to take action.

If you make a daily commitment to cutting back on bureaucracy, not only will your organization work faster, but this speed will become a major competitive advantage.

#8

KNOW THE FOUR KEY PILLARS FOR THE BUSINESS UNIT

For any department I am running, I manage four key pillars for the business unit.

- **Data:** What is all the data I need to track to improve performance? Is this data being visualized? Are the collection, organizing, and visualization of this data automated or manual?
- **People:** What people do I need? Are we holding the people we have highly accountable? Are the people we have highly engaged? Do our people have key performance indicators (KPIs)?
- **Systems:** What technologies do we need? Have we negotiated the tech we need? Are there new systems and technologies to replace old tech? Are the technologies all integrated together for ease of use, ease of reporting, and ease of tech execution?
- **Playbooks and processes:** What are the scripts and/or tasks that need to be executed? Do we have the scripts and playbooks for every scenario? Are all processes for any workflow highly documented and easy to follow?

Make sure you define, manage, and improve these four pillars to great management every day.

#9

PRIORITIZE TASKS AND PROJECTS

One of the most important things you can get right for your team is prioritizing the projects that drive maximum results.

When I was first building my software company, I spent a year at the ideation stage studying different strategies that would skyrocket my startup's growth. I became obsessed with nailing the 80/20 rule, which preaches maximizing your time and generating 80% of your needed results with 20% of your time. I would spend every morning obsessing over how to make every department efficient.

For any task across the whole company, I would rank and score on a scale from 1 to 5 (1 = Strong No, 2 = No, 3 = Neutral, 4 = Yes, 5 = Strong Yes):

- How does this rank at increasing new sales and customers?
- How does this rank at increasing usage?
- How does this rank at getting us to market?
- How does this rank at increasing demos?

Once I did this, I would make it a rule for every department to prioritize the tasks that ranked the highest.

When you want to identify the actions that are going to drive the greatest impact at your company, figure out what your rating variables are, from 1 to 5, for all your tasks. Then create a weighted scoring system. Lastly, prioritize important tasks for your team.

Pro tip: Limit your scoring variables to a maximum of five. If your team has to score a task for more than five variables, the likelihood that it will get done drops.

Once you define the variables, you want to give each variable a weight. For instance, you may weigh the following:

- **Sales:** 40%
- **Demos:** 20%
- **Users:** 10%
- **Impressions:** 10%
- **Effort (the time it takes to complete):** –20%

Effort is a big factor that can make a positive or a negative variable. For the tasks that score high and don't take a lot of time to complete, you want to score high.

Once you define your one to five variables that you want to score for team tasks, start scoring each task for each variable and then multiply it by the weighted score. You are then going to add up all the scores and *boom!* You have a weighted task list that ensures that your team works on the most important tasks.

I found it easier to score these features in a spreadsheet because it allowed me to do more customizing.

Keep in mind that although this is a foolproof method to figure out priorities, never forget that sometimes as a leader, you may have to listen to your instincts and complete a task that's considered "low priority."

For example, if I was delivering a keynote presentation that scored low on the to-do list, I might still place a lot of my time and resources on preparation because the returns on investment would be exponential. This presentation will put my brand in front of thousands, so that task would get moved up the priority ladder.

As you manage your team, prioritize tasks that will increase your team's success and ensure that you don't waste time on projects that don't move the needle.

#10

BREAK DOWN LARGE, HAIRY OBJECTIVES INTO SMALL, DOABLE TASKS

Have you ever set a huge goal for yourself, like losing a bunch of weight or saving up for a vacation, and it never ended up happening? Why do you think that is? It could be because you lacked the discipline or maybe the timing wasn't right.

But most likely you never completed those huge goals because instead of breaking them down into smaller tasks, you kept them as big, hairy goals. These goals were likely so big and intimidating that you had no idea where to begin. You just couldn't wrap your head around it. As a result, you kept putting off getting started.

When a target is too big, it's only human nature for people to shrug it off. But when you go all-in, you can't have this happen to your team because this means *zero* progress and *zero* initiative, and your people stay stuck in the same position.

Whenever a huge task or challenge hits your radar, you need to make it a habit to immediately start turning that objective into weekly and daily activities. Here's how you do that:

1. Break down the goal or project into smaller steps.
   This will help you figure out a concrete plan for how to crush the goal.
2. Rank those smaller steps in order of importance.
3. Delegate tasks to your team based on the skill set that's needed for the job.
   Make it clear to your people that even though you delegated the tasks, they are 100% responsible for their job and you expect them to crush it.
4. Give out deadlines to your team and stick to those deadlines.

Once you follow these steps, do regular check-ins to make sure everybody is on the same page, because for these big goals to come to fruition, there has to be cohesion and teamwork.

#11

WORK THE DEALS THAT ARE LIKELY TO CLOSE FIRST

As a leader, I always go down my task list and prioritize from the highest likelihood to close to the lowest likelihood to close. Let's say my priorities for the day are as follows: I've got a deal where I pitched them. They've got a contract. They love the deal. They're getting approval, and they just have to sign it.

I've also got three deals in negotiation and five deals in consultation, which means I pitched them, I'm following up, and I'm just waiting to hear back on the next steps. And lastly, I've got 100 leads for prospects.

I'm going to hit my three negotiating opps first: call, text, and email. Then I'm going to hit my consult opps and follow up to move them to consult, negotiator signed. Lastly, I'm hitting my cold outreach.

Always work your deals in the pipeline first before you go after cold opportunities.

#12

CREATE A GAME PLAN THE NIGHT BEFORE

I want you to start a nightly ritual where you spend time with your family and practice self-care (i.e. relax and unwind, get good sleep), but also make a game plan for how you're going to conquer the next day.

Every night, list all the priorities and tasks you want to complete in order of biggest impact to lowest impact, and greatest difficulty to least difficulty.

If you need to, make sure to also gather any documents and resources that you will need to complete your tasks so everything you need to crush the day is in the same place. In addition to this list, list any pain points you had from the previous day and come up with strategies to eliminate those pains.

Doing this every night will give you a clear roadmap of the upcoming day and ensure that you stick to your goals. This will also help you start your day out on a good note with focus and direction.

If you sketch out your priorities, identify your challenges (and how to overcome them), and gather the resources you need to crush the day, you will be more productive, feel less stressed out, and be empowered to smash your goals!

#13
CONSTANTLY COACH

A company is only as great as the revenue it drives month after month.

To ensure that your sales team is generating maximum revenue, you have to teach them the skills they need to close deals. This is why, out of all the responsibilities you have, coaching is by far one of the most important. But don't look at coaching as a one-and-done deal or something you do once a year, where you check off that task box and move on to other priorities.

Most people forget the information taught to them within a week. That's just how the human brain works. This is why if you want your people to retain the lessons you teach them, you need to do the following:

- **Constantly coach.**
  Shoot for weekly coaching sessions (30 to 60 minutes) where everyone on your team is required to attend. Depending on your resources and your workload, this can be tricky, but be consistent with your frequency. Employees learn the most when they can rely on a predictable training schedule.
  Also be proactive about your coaching. Instead of waiting for employees to come up to you with their problem, give priority to training underperformers.
- **Provide training across different channels** (one-on-ones, team stand-ups, etc.).
  Constantly reiterating key coaching points across channels makes the valuable information you share stick.
- **Be smart about the coaching curriculum.**

To elaborate on this point, let's consider sales coaching. Too much sales training focuses on overcoming sales objections. But what good is it to know how to handle an objection like "I'm not interested" or "Send me more information" if you don't know what to ask once you get past the objection? In this scenario, prioritizing discovery questions is crucial so that your people know how to properly qualify prospects.

Whether you're in sales or any other industry, you have to be strategic about what you're focusing on in your curriculum.

Lastly, make sure you let the data dictate what you cover in training. Use data to locate the weak areas your team has and zero in on those areas during training.

#14

HOST EFFECTIVE TEAM MEETINGS WITH EVERYONE

Here are some tips for how to host the most effective team meetings with anyone:

- **Set the intention for the meeting:** Share what the goal of the meeting is so everyone is on the same page. Establish ground rules for the meeting and share what the protocols are to ensure that everyone understands the problem you are trying to solve and the expected actions.

- **Be the mediator:** You want to act as the mediator to facilitate idea-sharing and ensure that everyone on the team contributes. As the mediator, refrain from sharing your own opinions so that you facilitate new ideas instead of influencing the team to do things your way.

- **Help the team withhold judgment and emotions:** Encourage each team member to refrain from reacting to any suggestions. The focus should be on getting as many unbiased recommendations as possible, not for anyone's ideas to get railroaded.

- **Finalize an action plan:** Conclude the meeting by expressing gratitude for the team's hard work and creating an action plan (assign roles and timelines). Schedule relevant follow-ups to ensure that collaboration runs smoothly and the project gets finalized.

#15

NO MEETING SHOULD LAST LONGER THAN 30 MINUTES

There are entirely too many meetings that take place every day in the professional world when more than half of them could be emails or texts.

This is why, if you must schedule a meeting (if there's no way around it), be strict about the time and keep your meetings to 30 minutes maximum. Thirty minutes is my magic number because it's the perfect amount of time to brainstorm a game plan or a solution to a pain point. Any longer than 30 minutes is too long and not only wastes your employees' time but costs the company money.

To stick to this time window, you have to keep the strictest agenda. Figure out what your main objective of the meeting is (you should already know this when you decide you need to have a meeting). Figure out what topics need to be discussed, in what order, and how much time you should dedicate to each topic on the agenda.

Write down the topics and the time you're going to allot to each issue and stick to it.

No exceptions!

#16

ASK BETTER QUESTIONS

As an all-in leader, you will often have such a lengthy task list that it will be hard to find time to come up for air.

Questioning your action plans can take you from constantly being in "Go mode" to working more strategically. So before you start running from one task to the next, pause and ask these questions about anything on your to-do list:

- What is the goal of this?
- Why am I working on this?
- What is the problem I am solving?
- Who benefits from this being solved?
- What could I be doing instead that drives bigger results for the company?

Everything you do has an opportunity cost, whether you are aware of it or not. When you factor in that cost, a seemingly productive activity could turn out to be a total waste of time.

So, ask better questions and prioritize high-impact and high-result activities first.

#17
LEARN FAST AND FAIL FAST

You always want to encourage your people to learn and improve every day. However, you don't want employees to take months to learn something just to have a bad outcome.

A poor outcome after a long learning cycle means you've wasted precious labor, time, and dollars you can't get back. You want to instead launch fast learning cycles, where employees are absorbing educational materials, skilling up quickly, and leveraging what they've learned quickly.

To teach fast, put together small, hands-on instructional groups and workshops, where employees can learn and practice the essential skills needed for their role. With this approach to education, if there's failure, it won't be as costly to your team.

Make the phrase "fail fast" one of your team mantras because it's always better to fail fast when the stakes and costs are low instead of failing late in the game.

#18

MAKE SURE YOUR REPS TAKE RESPONSIBILITY FOR TRAINING

Whether it's sales, recruitment, or any other department, most employees think that because they did the training they deserve an A for their efforts. Then when they fail, they blame the training, even though they haven't done the follow-up work of applying what they learned in training.

It's important to let your employees know: they are responsible for applying what they learn during training. They can take ownership by following these steps:

1. Pay attention in training.
2. Raise your hand with questions.
3. Take notes.
4. Get a study group to compare notes and actually study your notes afterward.
5. Do some homework and practice what you just learned.

I can offer no better advice for taking a company to the next level than owning your own development. Make sure to stress these steps during and after every training.

#19

GET GREAT TRAINERS AND SUPPORT THEM

If you hire a trainer to teach your team, it's still *your* job to make sure your reps *apply* what they learn.

#20
GET PAID OR PAY FOR IT

Teach your team that they will get paid in the future for the decisions, actions, and habits they make today or they will pay the price in the future for the lack of decisions, the lack of action, and the poor habits they practice today.

The choice is theirs.

Get paid for today or pay the price for today.

#21

COACH YOUR TEAM
ON SPECIFIC TASKS

Managers: "Do this, this way."
All-in leaders: "Tell me first how you would do it."

When you take the all-in approach, the rep gets to give their point of view first. The leader gets to see if any gaps exist in strategy, execution, skill set, or approach. Then the leader coaches on filling those gaps rather than solely instructing without understanding.

Be an all-in leader, not a bad manager.

#22

WORK WHERE YOU CAN HAVE
THE BIGGEST IMPACT

Instead of wasting your time on busy-work, be strategic and take on the tasks where you can make the biggest impact.

Regardless of whether it's in your area of expertise, if there's a huge bottleneck at your company and no one has resolved it, tackle that challenge. That's what makes the difference between managers and leaders who go all-in.

Managers are "by the book" about everything. They worry about the chain of command. And they won't touch an issue if it's not part of their job responsibilities. But a leader who goes all-in doesn't let anything keep them from using their natural talents wherever the company needs it the most.

So, learn your company's priorities, and choose challenges that push the greater mission forward.

#23
BIG GOALS REQUIRE BIG RESOURCES

If you are going to give people on your team a big number to hit, make sure you give them the support and the resources to beat it.

Don't be the manager who gives a massive target for your team to hit but no budget, no plan, no support, no training, and no guidance to make it happen.

That's a recipe for failure. Invest big in your people's success to achieve quantum goals.

#24
GIVE YOUR TEAM A HEAD START

With every project, the best managers use their instincts to give their team a leg up in successfully completing the task.

They spot problems well before they happen, and they delegate work to nip it in the bud and save their teammates the stress. They can also sniff out opportunities to grow as a team, find a niche, and gain an edge on the market even if their competitors have more resources and a bigger name.

Instincts and foresight are invaluable, and they help the most dynamic leaders set their people up for success.

The bigger the project, the more your team is going to need you to leverage those leadership instincts to give them a head start, so don't shrug off this responsibility as a manager.

In turn, the more teammates you can train and transform into leaders with great instincts, the more unstoppable your team is going to be.

#25

CUT TIMELINES
FOR PROJECTS IN HALF

If you give yourself a year to complete a project, it will take a year. But if you give yourself a week, it will take only a week.

Your workflow is always dictated by the time constraints that you put in place. When you are working with your team on any projects, whether they're big or small, cut the timeline in half, and then try to cut the timeline in half again.

This sounds extreme, but when you give yourself the narrowest timeline, you end up crushing the task faster than anyone would have expected.

#26

WORK HARD ON THE RIGHT THINGS VS. THE WRONG THINGS

Working on the right thing to maximize the results of your people has more impact than working hard on the wrong thing.

You get only about eight hours in the day, depending on how much you work. But often people are working hard on all the wrong things.

Be ruthless with prioritizing your task list based on greatest-impact and lowest-effort priorities. If you have one task that has an impact of 10 and an effort of 2 versus a task that has an impact of 10 and an effort of 8, always do the highest-impact, lowest-effort task first.

Work hard on the right things versus the wrong things.

#27

FIND THE BALANCE BETWEEN HELPING OTHERS AND MAINTAINING YOUR GOALS

To go all-in, you have to learn to be selfless and put your team ahead of yourself—constantly giving without expecting anything in return. This is the ideal way to operate, but it can undoubtedly have its pitfalls.

Constantly giving can leave you stressed out, mentally and emotionally drained, and completely behind with your own work. What's worse is that your peers can see your kindness as weakness and take advantage of you.

To avoid this worst-case scenario and reap the many benefits of giving (you, your team, and your company win when you choose to give), learn to find a balance between helping others and making your own goals a priority.

This means carving out time every day to tackle your goals.

If you make a point to use bi-weekly/monthly/quarterly one-on-ones as the designated space for your employees to get help from you, your team will know to look forward to these meetings to solve any bottlenecks or "stuck-ons" they're having instead of requesting your help around the clock.

You can also carve out your own "office hours" every week where your team can contact you with questions and problems. To avoid burnout, please make sure you stick to those office hours.

Lastly, give your team stretch tasks where they are forced to skill up so that when real problems arise, they are better equipped to handle them on their own without having to come to you for help.

If you follow these tips, you can be generous with your help and find the perfect balance with your own goals.

#28
SQUEEZE THE URGENCY WITH YOUR TEAM

If you want to set bigger goals and come up with a vision that takes your industry by storm, you have to start holding your team accountable and squeezing the urgency.

Shorten due dates not to increase pressure but to increase efficiency. If you want to scale like crazy and get a lot done in a short amount of time, create audacious deadlines, and actually stick to them.

#29

LOOK TO NEW EMPLOYEES FOR FRESH IDEAS

Managers stop growing when they stop listening to their people, especially the new employees. New employees are such an untapped resource at so many companies because when an organization hires someone new, the focus is always on training them for their role.

But in reality, new employees are a gold mine for fresh insights because they can give you completely impartial feedback. Think about it. A new employee has no attachment to the way things are normally done at your company. And because of this, they are better able to see what's working and not working so well.

So when you get a new employee, instead of rushing to get them accustomed to the company culture, ask for their feedback, their insights, and their ideas for how the company could improve and how you could be a better leader.

Be transparent with them. Let them know that as their manager you are always open to honest feedback, and you are constantly looking for ways to improve. This way the new employee feels free to give their genuine opinions and not just tell you what they think you want to hear.

Doing this will keep your leadership skills from going stale, and it will help the company continually level up.

#30

TEACH YOUR TEAM THE VALUE OF HARD WORK

If you don't go out there and put in the work, you're not going to get the results you want. If you don't go out there and put in the effort, you're not going to get the results you want.

Always teach the team if they don't prioritize, take action, and put in the work, they don't deserve to win because they need to earn it.

Everything in life is earned, not given. Work like the rent is due every day.

MONTH 6

THRIVING IN ADVERSITY WITH RESILIENCE, DISCIPLINE, AND A GROWTH MINDSET

#1

SUSTAIN A POSITIVE MINDSET (EVERY. SINGLE. DAY.)

If you want to become the best version of yourself, you have to be positive.

I try to live up to this ideal because, ultimately, you can't expect your people to stay positive if you yourself are always pessimistic. From my experience, one of the biggest challenges is sticking to it every day and remaining positive no matter what. When you have bad days and it seems like everything is going wrong, it's easy to be negative, but it's so difficult to maintain an optimistic outlook.

So how do you sustain a positive mindset every single day, even on the hard days?

You fake it until you make it.

This means that on tough days when nothing is going your way, smile. Put on your favorite music. Go outside and get some fresh air and sunshine.

Even if you woke up today in a crappy mood, if you take these actions, they will take you from fake positivity to genuinely feeling better on the inside and the outside. Never forget that you have control over your attitude, and the actions you take will make or break a positive mindset.

So, choose positivity every day. And if you have to, fake it until you make it to get through the most difficult days. Your team will pick up on your energy and emulate it because positivity breeds positivity.

#2

DO WIT: WHATEVER IT TAKES

One of the fundamental principles I've preached at Seamless. AI since the beginning is doing Whatever It Takes (WIT) to crush it.

No matter what hurdles life throws your way. No matter what the stats say. No matter what the naysayers argue. WIT means going all out with the resources you have to make the impossible possible.

Teach your team to bring a WIT attitude to every new challenge they face. Regardless of their job title, salary, or experience, every person on the team has to be willing to do WIT to WIN.

If there are any bad habits, doubts, negative beliefs, or toxic people in your team's network that would prevent them from doing WIT, work with them to break those obstacles down and get them back on track.

Additionally, one of the best ways to quickly teach your team how to leverage a WIT mindset is to have them read my book *Whatever It Takes: Master the Habits to Transform Your Business, Relationships, and Life*.

Whatever It Takes teaches hundreds of habits to help your team hone their agency and maximize their success. Pick up a copy and help your team bring that relentless WIT mindset to every aspect of their personal and professional lives.

#3

THE RICHES ARE IN THE CONSISTENT WORK NICHES

To accomplish anything amazing in this world, it takes relentless hard work every day.

If you want to generate results in sales, you have to prospect every day, no matter what. If you want to hire 100 new employees, you have to recruit candidates every day, no matter what. Everything you want in life, from that dream car to that dream house, are all on the other side of hard work. The riches are in the consistent hard work niches.

It can be boring doing the same thing day in and day out. But if you can turn the monotony into breakthrough success, you will make all of your team's goals and dreams a reality.

Consistency creates compounding long-term success.

#4
IMPROVE BY 1% EVERY DAY

A huge myth with management is that the greatest leaders join a company, and their leadership is so radical, they seemingly take the team from 0 to 180 degrees overnight.

While it's great to look up to this myth as an ideal, the greatest managers have small but frequent wins and make 1% improvements every day rather than huge sweeping victories.

Every single day I tell my team how important it is to improve by 1% every single day. It's one of my foundational principles because it illustrates the power of tiny yet consistent progress.

Think about it. . .if you were to improve by 1% for every workday for a year, by the time you got to the end of the year, you would improve by 37× from where you started.

If you want to make a huge, 180-degree transformation in your career, your health, your finances, or your relationships, you don't have to make dramatic changes to your routine overnight. You just have to make small goals and small improvements, and over time the returns for your effort will be tenfold.

To leverage the 1% rule, set a goal for yourself and every day create a list of specific, minor tasks you can do to chip away at the bigger goal.

Make it a point to make some kind of progress every single day, whether it's making a few extra phone calls, finding a few extra leads, or scheduling a few extra interviews (it all depends on the goal, of course).

Consistency is key with the 1% rule.

If you focus on making some kind of progress every day, you will eventually crush the goal no matter how big it is.

#5

GROWTH COMES FROM CHALLENGES

Teach your team to believe that challenges are the blessings and keys for growth.

Don't ask, "Why is this happening to me?" Instead ask, "Why is this happening *for* me?" Little adjustments like that will help change your team's perspective and their view on life.

Instead of being negative about challenges, embrace them because opportunity and growth come from challenges.

- Learn from every failure.
- Grow from every problem.
- Never play the victim.
- Take action.
- Try your best.

#6

GRIT HAS NOTHING TO DO WITH WINNING

Grit is about pushing through when things go sideways.

It means finding a way when you hit a brick wall, no matter what it takes. Like prospecting after hours even though you're tired. Or pushing through ridiculous late-stage objections in a big deal. Or refusing to quit even though you heard "no" 13 times in a single day.

Talent doesn't make you gritty.

In fact, those with the most grit usually aren't the most talented people in the room. They just work harder than the rest even when things don't go their way.

Winning happens every once in a while. But grit happens every day, even if you don't see it on a dashboard.

#7

SDB: "SHOW, DO, BE"

Lead your team to success using this secret SDB leadership framework:

- **Show** up every day giving it everything you've got.
- **Do** the work without complaining.
- **Be** positive about the opportunity regardless of what the critics say.

#8

KNOW YOUR WORTH

One of the things that kills a team's potential is self-rejection.

Many people on your team won't become the greatest they can be because they doubt themselves or let the fear of failure hold them back, so they stay reserved.

Don't think you deserve the promotion? Apply for it anyway.

Don't think that one person will give you advice? Ask for it anyway.

Don't think that idea is good enough? Share it anyway.

Don't think they will take your call? Make it anyway.

Don't think that strategy is good enough? Test it anyway.

Don't think you are ready for the new position? Take it anyway.

Coach the team to stop the doubt and self-rejection and do IT anyway, whatever IT is.

Mindset over matter.

#9

NO ONE KNOWS WHAT THEY ARE DOING AT FIRST

Teach your team that their fear of looking dumb is holding them back in their career.

We never know what we are doing when we get started, so embrace a beginner's mindset. Anyone who starts anything doesn't know what they are doing at first. But over time, they get better and better.

Kill those ridiculous fears and just get started today.

#10

TEAMWORK MAKES THE DREAM WORK

Make sure everyone knows that you're all a team. You win as a team, and you lose as a team.

When one person struggles, we all struggle. When one person wins, we all win.

#11

TEACH YOUR TEAM THAT IT'S "YOU VS. YOU"

If you want to go all-in and become the best that you can be, you have to get laser-focused on your mindset.

Why? Because your mindset is the one thing you have absolute control over.

If you have big goals for yourself professionally and personally, guess what could come between you and those goals? It's not any one person or any one thing; it's a negative mindset.

Ask your team today to think about whether they have a positive or negative mindset. Do they fill their mind and network with positive thoughts, people, actions, and beliefs or negative ones?

It's so important to reflect on your mindset because no matter what happens, it's always you versus you.

Surround yourself with the positive.

- Positive thoughts
- Positive actions

- Positive people
- Positive habits
- Positive beliefs
- Positive reinforcement

Never forget that the number-one reason people succeed or fail is their mindset.

It's you vs. you.

#12

MAKE ROOM FOR RISKS

Whatever industry you're in, I can guarantee that what it looks like today is different from what it looked like a month ago.

Every industry goes through constant change that you have to anticipate and account for. Plus, to add to the stress, if you work for a small startup, you've probably had slim quarters or even slim years where you're not raking in much profit.

A company that thrives through all this instability is one where the leaders make their people feel protected from these pitfalls. This means building a space where employees can be creative and take risks without fear of punishment or losing their job.

Back in 2020, when the world was in quarantine and a lot of companies were laying off their talent to save their bottom line, we made it a policy at Seamless.AI to make our people our number-one priority, and we didn't lay off anyone that year.

In retrospect, not only was 2020 a record-breaking year for Seamless. AI, but we earned the loyalty of a lot of our employees.

Take that little anecdote as a lesson that to build the greatest team, you don't have to put together a dream team. All you have to do is make your people feel protected and they will go all out for you.

#13

AS YOUR TEAM CHANGES, ENCOURAGE YOUR PEOPLE TO BE PROACTIVE AND PICK UP THE SLACK

In today's job market, teams are constantly changing.

With people moving from job to job at lightning speed, you may have a dream team during Q1, and by the end of Q3, the team looks completely different, with resignations and new hires.

If this sounds familiar, then you probably spend a lot of time recruiting and onboarding. With all this catch-up work, there's no time to get tactical and play offense with competitors.

So to stay ahead of competitors, it's imperative that all employees go beyond their roles and assume leadership responsibilities when there are team changes. This means taking initiative, completing and shipping projects ASAP, and making final decisions without being asked.

Taking up leadership responsibilities can be challenging for employees who have no desire to become a leader. But to encourage these team members, remind them that stepping up is only temporary but absolutely crucial to the success of the team.

Teams will change—that's an inevitability of today's workforce—but prepare your people to take up the slack and assume leadership responsibilities when they must.

#14

DON'T HATE, IMITATE!

Train your individual contributors not to hate on top performers.

Top performers have learned the secrets, systems, processes, and playbooks to be successful. Instead of hating on them, learn from them!

Teach the team to learn from the top performers because that top performer is right where the rest of the team is trying to be.

Model what the best do. And remember: don't hate, imitate!

#15

TEACH THE IMPORTANCE OF CURIOSITY

Curiosity in business is all about being open and eager to always learn new strategies and secrets to improve. Curiosity teaches you to try to always seek new answers to improve. . .and learn new things to maximize performance.

Coach your team to be curious:

- Curious about what they don't know
- Curious about how much they can learn
- Curious about how much better they can become

Past performance is a static view of where you have been.

Curiosity is a view of where you can go.

#16

MAKE BIG ISSUES SEEM SMALL

Failure is inevitable.

But the next time your team has a setback, don't criticize or punish your people. The reality is, if your team has failed, their spirits are already down. More than likely they are already beating themselves up enough as it is. Your criticism will just add fuel to the fire.

When failure happens, what people really need is encouragement. So, inspire your people. Remind them that mistakes happen. Motivate them to learn from their failure and turn it into a comeback. Talk about how easy the mistake is to fix and bounce back from. This shifts your employees' mindsets, and they go from doubting their abilities to believing that not only can they overcome this setback, but it will be a breeze to do.

#17
SHOOT YOUR SHOT

Teach your team to take chances and shoot their shot even if they are scared of missing the game-winning basket. Make it safe for your people to always take action and fail forward if they do not succeed because if they aren't taking risks, they will never accomplish their full potential.

Michael Jordan famously said, "I've missed more than 9,000 shots in my career. I've lost almost 300 games. Twenty-six times I've been trusted to take the game-winning shot and missed. I've failed over and over and over again in my life. And that is why I succeed."

Make your team environment a safe place to take chances, shoot shots, and maximize potential. And if your team members miss or fail, coach them to learn from the data from that mistake, fail forward, and do better the next time around.

People who feel safe to shoot shots will perform better, generate more results, and be happier overall.

#18
TEACH TENACITY

Coach your people to always be tenacious.

You may not be great at your job, know the product well, or understand how to best serve the customer, but if you keep at it, despite all the rejection you get, you will eventually figure it out and succeed.

#19
BECOME THE PRESSURE MAGNET

Become the pressure magnet for your team. As the pressure comes in from different leaders or departments, develop strategies and execution plans to fill the gaps and maximize the team's success.

When you go all-in, you want to minimize the pressure for your team, rather than place more pressure on your employees.

#20
TEACH COACHABILITY

Coachability is your ability to take in constructive feedback without getting offended.

The trick to coachability is that your desire to get better needs to be bigger than your ego. When your passion to grow is greater than your pride, your growth potential is limitless. One way I teach coachability is by sharing a story about how I lost $4,000,000 running my second company, EnMobile.

I started my first company when I was 18, and it generated more than $12 million in sales. Because of this early success, I got cocky, and when I launched my second company, EnMobile, I was highly uncoachable. I didn't listen to investors, experts, or mentors because I thought I knew everything.

As you can imagine, the outcome was disastrous. I lost everything in four years, and I was flat-out broke. I learned a valuable lesson from this failure, and I told myself I would stay coachable and hungry to learn from anyone for the rest of my life.

Teach your people to avoid massive failures by remaining humble because when they're coachable they can learn everything they need to succeed in their career.

#21
EMBRACE YOUR VULNERABILITIES

No leader is perfect, so showcase your flaws to the team. Let them know that imperfections are completely OK and don't get in the way of pushing the team's success.

The reason I stress this is because people embrace leaders who are vulnerable and human, just like them. When you embrace your vulnerabilities and show your team how human you are, it becomes easier to connect with them.

Being transparent about your weaknesses breaks down the wall between you and your team.

#22
ASK FOR IN-PERSON FEEDBACK

In-person feedback is one of my favorite ways to receive constructive criticism because it's the most immediate and actionable. When you're asking an employee for feedback in person, they don't have time to craft a "safe" response that feeds your ego.

There are very real benefits to asking for feedback in person, but it can be awkward for employees to be forthcoming with you. To avoid this, make your feedback request about you, the employee, and their improvement.

Something along the lines of, "What do you need from me in order to keep getting better?" Or, "How can I support you better?"

Next is the most important step: once you make this request, *be quiet*!

If you say anything to try to diffuse the situation (i.e. "No big deal, though" or "Just thought I'd ask"), the employee is going to assume your request isn't serious, and they'll just give you some phony answer. So give them the floor to speak their mind.

Once they're done, accept the feedback and act on what you hear.

When the employee can see you actually changing, they'll know that you took them seriously, and this will encourage them to continue being transparent with their feedback.

#23
NEVER SAY "I CAN'T DO IT"

Teach the team to never say "I can't do it" and instead to say "How can I do it?"

Whatever the end goal, the most unstoppable teams strive to find a way to crush it. Forbid the team from saying "I can't," and instead teach the team to say "How can I do it?"

You'd be surprised how just a slight shift in language can become an incredible mindset shift.

#24
DIVIDE AND CONQUER
BIG PROJECTS

The first time I was reminded of this secret was when we were building a new feature here at Seamless.AI.

I pulled in 10–15 developers to work on this feature around the clock because I thought it would help us roll out the feature faster for our clients. Unfortunately, everyone started working over each other. There was a lot of miscommunication, and it was utter chaos.

The next time around, when we worked on another feature, we scaled down to four people, and this smaller team finished the feature in record time. I told myself I would never put a whole team on a big project again and would instead have a small SWAT team divide and conquer the task at hand.

For any project, large or small, keep the execution team small, and divvy up tasks to get it across the finish line with the highest quality, lowest cost, and greatest strategy. When the team is small, task management and communication are all easier to execute.

As a rule of thumb, always remember that the larger the team, the longer it will take to complete the project.

#25
TURN MISTAKES INTO LEARNING LESSONS

Whenever an employee makes mistakes, instead of getting upset and playing the blame game, take their mistake and use it as a learning opportunity for the whole team.

Depending on the scale of the mistake, sit with the employee in a one-on-one and do a deep-dive into what went wrong.

Figure out what actions they could have taken to avoid the mistake.

Then share this information with the rest of the team without making an example out of the employee (make them anonymous if you have to and just focus on the issue that was resolved).

When you immediately pinpoint what went wrong and share your insights with the team, this builds trust between you and the employee.

They can rest assured that when things go left, they can turn to you for help. They don't have to sweep the mistake under the rug and hide it from you because they're afraid of the repercussions.

When you turn mistakes into teachable moments, you create an environment where learning is prioritized over fear and punishment.

#26

SPEND TIME ON PROBLEMS VS. SOLUTIONS

Leaders who go all-in spend 10% of their time on the problem and 90% of their time on figuring out the solution.

Identify the problem, and don't point fingers or play the blame game. Try to understand the intricacies of the problem, and when your employees bring up issues, don't beat them up for it because it will backfire and your team will never share any problems with you.

Once you've identified the problem, spend 90% of your time coming up with an execution plan to solve the problem.

#27

WHAT DO YOU NEED TO DO TODAY?

What is one thing that comes to your mind as a leader that you know you need to do today?

Maybe it's:

- Sitting in on calls to coach your people
- Having a tough conversation with an under-performer
- Coaching the team to increase their activity
- Sourcing and hiring someone you desperately need on the team to fill a talent gap
- Giving a raise to a game changer on the team
- Creating scalable templates
- Firing a toxic team member
- Helping the team solve a problem or complete a project

Whatever it is, take time today to do that one task you've been procrastinating on. Whatever it takes.

Today is the day to get it done.

#28
SUCCESS IS UNCOMFORTABLE

You have to get comfortable being uncomfortable if you ever want to be successful.

Coach your team that growth comes from discomfort. If you stay in your comfort zone, that is where you will fail. Being too comfortable in your situation is never good. You always have to strive for more.

Be *proud* of where you are at but never *satisfied*. Have the *hunger* to achieve more and be more. Never settle.

Success is uncomfortable, so get comfortable with the discomfort of growth.

#29
BET ON HARD WORK, NOT LUCK

Teach your team that the key to everything is hard work.

Hard work gives you a scalable, predictable, and repeatable system for future success. Luck gives you one tiny win or special moment in time that you'll never repeat.

Instead of betting on luck, bet on hard work. Because the harder you work, the luckier you will get.

#30
ENJOY THE JOURNEY

Coach your people that the key to life is to be happy with what they have, while they work for what they want.

This is one of the hardest things for people, especially overachievers, to get right. But it will help everyone enjoy the journey to success versus being miserable on the journey.

PART III

THE KEYS TO UNLOCKING YOUR
TEAM'S POTENTIAL

MONTH 7

THE ART OF COMMUNICATION, TRANSPARENCY, AND ACTIVE LISTENING

#1
ACTIVE LISTENING IS ALL-IN LEADERSHIP

If you are going to take the time to meet with people, truly listen to them. When you leverage active listening and ignore distractions, you show how much you value your team's time and ideas.

Active listening is a core aspect of going all-in. And when you have meetings or one-on-ones, you can practice active listening by:

- Closing out all the tabs on your computer
- Muting your phone
- Taking notes
- Muting yourself and refraining from interrupting employees
- Asking meaningful follow-up questions for clarification

If you're virtual, record the call to play it back, catch any key points you missed, and most importantly pay attention to how you interact with others. (Are you giving people the space to share their ideas, or are you talking over everyone?)

Speak in such a way that others love to listen to you, and listen in such a way that others love talking to you.

#2
BE TRANSPARENT

Transparency is pivotal for team members to have the information they need to make the right decisions that move the business forward. But keep in mind that transparency doesn't mean sharing every little detail of every decision.

When leadership makes a decision, share the context for the decision so the team can understand why this was the move to make, and keep rolling!

#3

MAKE YOUR EXPECTATIONS CRYSTAL CLEAR

We all have been here before. Your manager gives you an assignment that's pretty open-ended. You put in your best effort and complete the project, only for your manager to furiously send it back because it's not what they wanted.

Who's in the wrong here? The employee? Or the manager?

If you said the manager, you are correct! It's great to give your people open-ended assignments where they have to get proactive, fill in the gaps, and come up with a finished product without much instruction.

This teaches your employees to think and work independently without you holding their hand and micromanaging their every move.

But, if you assign a project or a task and you have a sense of what you want to see and what you don't want to see, don't play games here! Be clear about what exactly it is that you want, and then give your people the freedom to use their talent and skills to bring your vision to reality.

In the end, you will get the quality you expected, and your team will have more confidence knowing that they crushed it!

#4

MASTER THE ART
OF COMMUNICATION

To become the world's greatest all-in leader, the most important skill you need is communication.

The greatest leaders perfect the art of communication. Bad managers, by contrast, crash and burn because they never learn how to effectively communicate. If you want to crush it at your company, follow these rules when it comes to communication (make sure you study them until you can repeat them back verbatim):

- **Keep it simple:** If you aren't clear about what you want, your team won't be able to execute. Don't overcomplicate things. Keep your requests simple and be concise at all times.
- **Be decisive:** There's nothing worse than a manager who can't make up their mind. On Monday they want one thing, and by Tuesday they've done a 180. Being indecisive wastes time and money. Know what you want and be consistent.
- **Be respectful:** As a manager, you are a direct representation of your company. Because of this, always show the utmost respect to everyone, especially your team.

Never take your communication habits for granted. Your team will observe how you communicate and follow your lead.

Always be mindful of what you say and how you say it, and remember that communication is a two-way street. Encourage your people to lead the conversations and listen.

#5

COMMUNICATE USING CLARITY, PURPOSE, AND TRUST

When you are communicating with your team, do it with clarity, purpose, and trust.

- **Clarity:** Make sure your people are so clear on what's expected of them that they can act without needing permission or assistance from superiors.
- **Purpose:** Make sure that your people understand why they are working on a task and how it contributes to the mission and vision of the company.
- **Trust:** Make sure your people know they can depend on you and that they feel safe working with you.

Whenever you communicate, follow the rules of clarity, purpose, and trust to build up your team.

#6

BECOME OBSESSED WITH PEOPLE AND HOW THEY THINK

It sounds cliché, but to improve in management, you have to be a people person.

When I say, "people person," I'm not just talking about socializing. I'm talking about studying the psychology of people.

Learn what people want the most in life.

- What makes people tick?
- What motivates people?
- What discourages people?

Knowing the answers to these kinds of questions is key to helping your employees generate results that push their career forward.

I would advise you to pick up a couple of psychology books to learn more because psychology is a big part of leadership, but here's a summary of my own observations as a 20-year leader:

- No one cares about you and how accomplished and intelligent you are. People care about what you can do for them.
- Even though we all love the idea of independence, no one achieves success alone. Any accomplishments you've ever achieved were the result of support from other people.
- Letting a person know that they can win and accomplish whatever goal or task they have in front of them is one of the most powerful things you can do. Showing your faith in a person's abilities is all they need to thrive.

#7

LOSING TOP TALENT HAS A PRICE

Too many leaders think that their people are replaceable. Too many leaders overestimate what new people can do and underestimate how valuable their current people are. I sincerely believe that my team members are irreplaceable.

You need to believe the same about your people, too.

If you fully believe the people on your team are irreplaceable, you will do everything in your power to unleash their potential and maximize their success. Value your people and keep them happy, even if it means raises, recognition, support, coaching, etc.

If you have top talent, do whatever it takes to maximize their success and keep them happy. Don't lose your top people or you will pay the price.

#8

PEOPLE WANT TO FEEL SEEN AND UNDERSTOOD

The one thing that everybody wants the most is to feel seen and understood. If you can manage to make your people feel heard and understood, they will show the utmost loyalty to you.

Here are a couple of ways that you can make your people feel seen:

- Remember the names of every person you come into contact with at your organization.
  This sounds simple enough, but people love hearing their own name. It's a part of who they are and their identity. Remembering someone's name makes them feel an immediate connection to you. So come up with a method like memorization or name association to remember people's names.
- Get people to talk about themselves and actively listen.
  Get your people to talk about themselves, their interests, their hobbies, you name it. Ask questions about things they are proud of, their greatest achievements, and so on.

The most important thing is that when your people tell you about themselves, you need to show genuine interest. This will earn their trust because people are the proudest of their successes, and they love getting the opportunity to brag about their accomplishments to a genuinely engaged listener.

#9

LISTEN TO YOUR EMPLOYEES' PROBLEMS

Whenever an employee comes to you with a complaint, listen to them and let them do the talking.

Talking over them because you want to be right or show off your expertise likely won't get the problem solved, and it will just make your employee reluctant to ever come to you again if they have other issues in the future.

So, listen to what they say, show sincere concern, and encourage them to be fully transparent. This will build trust and give the employee the chance to use you as a soundboard for their problems.

You'll find that a lot of times when you give your employee plenty of space to talk, not only will they arrive at the answers to their own problems, but they will be grateful to have someone to turn to when they need support.

#10
MAKE SURE EVERYONE IS HEARD AT MEETINGS

In team meetings, it's easy for a select few to take over the entire conversation, while the rest of the group stays silent for the majority of the time.

You want to avoid this because the key to going all-in is consulting and leveraging input from a diverse number of voices. Try these tips to guarantee that every time you have a meeting everyone is getting the time and opportunity to give their input:

- Draft a clear plan for the meeting ahead of time and share it with the team. Don't include just the purpose of the meeting but also the questions you want to discuss. Sharing questions ahead of time gives team members who tend to be quiet or not the best at thinking off the cuff the necessary time to prepare some answers.
- Just like your morning stand-ups, take the time to recognize every individual in the meeting. This releases the tension and puts everyone at ease. Remember, feeling comfortable is key to participation.

- Whenever you get a bunch of people with different personalities in the same room, people are going to talk over each other. It's inevitable. When this happens, never forget that as the manager, you are the moderator. Whenever you have a situation where two employees start talking over each other, always give the floor to the employee who is the more junior of the two because, again, the goal here is to empower a diversity of voices.
- With every meeting, make sure that every single person has a chance to speak at least once.

#11
DON'T OVERSHARE

Transparency is a word that gets thrown around a lot because it's so important to efficiency as well as relationship building. But this term gets used so much I think its true meaning has been lost.

Despite what's commonly discussed, as a manager, transparency doesn't mean overloading your people with information that isn't important to their job position. Transparency instead means sharing key decisions, wins, and losses that are vital to the company mission.

Rather than divulge every little detail, share only these two essentials:

- **The reasoning for the decision:** Maybe the company is experiencing a bottleneck pain, and this decision will resolve that. Whatever the rationale is for a big decision, let employees know what that reasoning is.
- **The potential impact of the decision:** Be honest with your employees, and let them know the possible impact, whether it's good or bad.

Being transparent with your employees strengthens your relationships and helps your people work with a more informed focus. When your people are aware of key decisions, they know how important they are to the company. Just make sure not to overshare irrelevant details.

Share only the rationale and the impact.

#12

DON'T BE A ONE-UPPER: SUPPORT THE SUCCESS AND WINS OF YOUR TEAM

When someone tells you about a win, you can respond in two ways. You can celebrate and put a spotlight on the other person or you can turn the spotlight on yourself.

Here are some examples of turning the spotlight on yourself:

Employee says: I saw this movie Saturday, and it was awesome!

Manager says: Cool. I saw the Rotten Tomatoes reviews and heard it wasn't good.

Employee says: I went to Clearwater Beach this weekend. It was awesome.

Manager says: I've been to Clearwater. But I prefer Siesta Key because the restaurants and people are so much better.

So what's the problem? When you turn the spotlight back on you, you're subconsciously saying to your team member, "That's cool, but my experience is more interesting than yours."

Instead of making everything about you, keep the spotlight on the other person and build rapport. Here's what rapport-building responses look like:

"That sounds amazing! What was the best part for you?"

When you keep the spotlight on the other person, you're saying, "Your story matters. I care," and this simple gesture is the empathy your employees are looking for from you.

#13
WHAT'S ON YOUR MIND?

One of the best questions to ask when hosting a one-on-one meeting with every team member is:

"What's on your mind?"

This question opens the floodgates to hear the good, the bad, the ugly, and anything standing in the way of success. You're likely going to hear a number of personal and professional issues. Your only job is to listen intently and try to help them overcome any issues they've been having.

The genius with this question is that it's simple and open-ended, so it really gives your employees the chance to share more about what's going on with them.

You nurture your relationships with this question, which is what dynamic leadership is all about.

#14
DO NOT GLORIFY BURNOUT

Yes, success takes an insane amount of hard work, positivity, discipline, coachability, and doing whatever it takes to be successful. However, if someone on your team is feeling overwhelmed in their job, they need to talk to you as their manager. And if talking with you doesn't help, then they need to have a conversation with human resources.

Employees who burn out or don't feel heard end up churning. The best way to avoid burnout is to encourage your people to speak up when they feel overwhelmed, exhausted, or uninspired. Encourage your people to take action when things aren't going well.

We are all human, and bringing your people up when they are down is one of the greatest keys to success.

#15

GIVE YOUR PEOPLE THE BENEFIT OF THE DOUBT

We've all been here before. You set out to do something and you had the best of intentions. You might have been trying to help someone else out or help the company out. But despite your intentions, things end up blowing up in your face, and your efforts turn out to be a complete disaster.

Every time this happened, what did you want the people around you to do? You likely wanted them to look past the disaster, focus on your intentions, and give you the benefit of the doubt, right?

As an all-in leader, you need to learn to give to your team the same kindness and patience that you would hope to receive if you were in the same situation.

Too often, what creates static on teams are managers who've forgotten what it was like to be in their employees' shoes. They've spent so much time in a leadership role that they've forgotten about the countless mistakes they made and the many times their team leaders extended kindness.

Every day, you want to put yourself in your employees' shoes, remember what it was like to be in their position, and be the manager you would have wanted. Treat your team the way you would have wanted to be treated.

If you stick to this basic principle, there will be greater trust, and your relationships with your teammates will flourish.

#16
BE YOUR BIGGEST CRITIC

If you want to encourage your people to be forthcoming with their feedback, the ball is in your court. You have to start the constructive criticism, and they will follow your lead.

Instead of waiting for your employees to reach out to you with their thoughts and ideas for improvement, during team meetings and one-on-ones, call out your own mistakes when they come up.

Drawing attention to your shortcomings lowers the wall between manager and employee, makes you more human to your employees, and communicates your passion for the team and the company.

#17
TURN YOUR "WHY" INTO A PASSION STATEMENT

We talked about finding your "why" in Month 4. With this secret, I want you to turn your "why" into a one-sentence passion statement that you can read every day. Memorize it to the point where you can repeat it word for word.

Here's an example of a passion statement:

> My "why" is to make lead generation faster, easier, and more accurate to positively impact a billion people.

This is a great passion statement because

- It's clear.
- It's an action statement.
- It illustrates a higher purpose greater than myself.

#18

OPEN FEEDBACK

Ask for feedback early and often from your team.

When you ask for feedback, make sure you understand what is going well and what needs improvement. As you strive to get feedback, rather than position the request as a command, point out that you are working to maximize their potential and build a great place to work.

Whenever I ask for feedback, I let our whole company know that I want to do whatever it takes to help them realize their potential, but without their feedback, I don't know if I am doing a great job or a bad job.

This helps inspire people on the team to share. Now the big caveat to the feedback request is that you must have an open mind, and you can't overreact when you get feedback.

If you really want to get good feedback, don't respond; just think about why this person is sharing this information and how you can act on this feedback. There is a reason they are sharing this info with you.

So, don't react or respond to negative feedback in that moment. Get all the feedback and then give it a few days to review privately and brainstorm solutions.

#19

EMPIRES ARE DESTROYED FROM WITHIN

Identify the toxic employees at your company who are dragging your team down.

As soon as you locate these pain points, get rid of these people fast because they are toxic to the success of your team and the company.

The reason you want to get rid of toxic employees as fast as possible is because the longer that they stick around, the more damage they're going to cause.

A toxic employee lowers team morale and keeps others from producing their best work. If you want to unlock the full potential of your team, you need to find the toxic employees and remove them before they poison the entire company.

This will only strengthen your team in the long run.

And it will also let everyone know that you have zero tolerance for mediocrity, which will attract new top talent.

#20
CREATE A "NO EXCUSES" POLICY

I've worked with a plethora of unsuccessful people and individual contributors who always play the victim.

- Didn't finish the project? Nothing they could do about it.
- Missed their sales goals? Wasn't their fault.
- Not doing enough marketing activity? It's because they were waiting on a team member.
- Not enough new hires? The culture needs to be improved.
- Behind on goal? That's just the way it is.

These people always had an excuse for everything because they looked for problems instead of solutions. Anyone who consistently makes excuses or blames others for their lack of success will never be successful. This is why it's critical to coach your team to have a "no excuses" policy.

The key to success is to always look for solutions, not problems, and to rise up to the responsibility, not back down and run away.

Here is an example of a "no excuses" individual contributor:

> Didn't finish the project? How could I manage this project better? What people could I bring in to help? Where did we get stuck and how do we ensure it doesn't happen again?

> Missed sales goals? How could I improve the top of the funnel to create more opportunities? How could I make more calls, emails, appointments, and sales? How could I give better sales discovery and pitching to increase my close rate next time?

> Not doing enough marketing activity? How can I better partner with marketing to help generate more leads? What could I post on social media to help us get the word out about how we are serving the customers? What customer stories can I collect to give to marketing for social proof to acquire more customers?

> Not enough new hires? What can I do to prospect talent to join us? How can I share my story to help our recruiting team source more people?

> Behind on goal? What can I change qualitatively or quantitatively to catch up and beat the plan?

The more problems you solve, the greater your chances of success. The more excuses you make, the lower your chances of success. The "no excuses" policy is a game changer for your team and will encourage your team members to proactively take ownership of their success.

#21
EXPECT THE BEST FROM YOUR PEOPLE 100% OF THE TIME

Accept nothing but the absolute best from your people. And if they aren't at a place where they're able to produce their best work, coach them and challenge them until they are. Also, pay attention to any obstacles or blockers that may be keeping your employees from producing their best work.

A lot of times people may be afraid to do more than the bare minimum because they don't want to stick their necks out. If something goes wrong or results are lower than what was expected, they don't want to be punished or, worse, lose their job.

To avoid this, make it clear that employees will not be punished if their best work doesn't yield the best outcomes. Sometimes you put your best effort forward, and it amounts to nothing. Sometimes failure happens and it's completely out of your control.

Make this reality clear to your people and draw a line between fantastic work and the results of those efforts.

If your people produce quality work and see a bad outcome that's out of their control, don't hold it against them. Uplift them, and create an environment where the entire team is motivating each other when bad outcomes happen instead of pointing the finger.

#22
DON'T BE AFRAID TO HAVE DIFFICULT CONVERSATIONS

As a manager, from time to time you're going to have those difficult talks with your employees.

Maybe you have an employee who hasn't met quota for months. Maybe you need to let an employee go so they can move on to other career opportunities where they are a better fit. These are all very real situations that happen at companies all the time.

A lot of managers don't know how to handle these issues, and they don't know what to say without hurting somebody's feelings or burning a bridge.

Even though these conversations can be awkward, the good news is, we have the strategies to help you master them:

- **Handle tough conversations privately one-on-one:** It's always better to coach up and have difficult conversations with underperformers privately in a one-on-one. Try to keep group meetings and conversations all about good news, priorities, and KPIs, and hold conversations about low performance during one-on-ones.
- **Prepare:** When you're discussing a difficult issue, it's easy to get overwhelmed and forget key points. To avoid this, plan ahead. Put together an outline of the talking points you want to cover. Run through them ahead of time, so when you sit with the employee, you have maximum confidence.
- **Be crystal clear:** Tough situations require you to be intentional about the words you choose. In other words, don't beat around the bush. Be clear and concise and address the elephant in the room head on.
- **Actively listen:** Once you've made your case, give your employee a chance to respond, and actively listen to what they have to say.
- **Come up with a game plan:** Depending on the situation, work with the employee. Come up with a game plan and a timeframe to resolve the problem. Working with the employee will hold them accountable, make them responsible for resolving the problem, and help them grow.

#23
DEVELOP PIPs

I know performance improvement plans (PIPs) have a bad reputation with employees, but the goal of a PIP is to help team members improve and change the trajectory of their success.

Point this out to your entire team or company. Bad bosses use PIPs to stop investing in employees and fire them as quickly as possible. But leaders who go all-in use PIPs to create the urgency to improve and make the needed changes to succeed.

Remember, if an all-in leader has to fire people on a PIP, they will lose tens of thousands of dollars from all the time, effort, and money invested in recruiting, hiring, and training new talent.

Having to fire someone who you saw potential in is always the worst-case scenario. But sometimes a PIP has to be used as a last resort when you've tried everything else with an employee.

So when you put together a PIP, make a clear action plan to generate change, and make it your goal to help that team member thrive.

#24

DEAL WITH CONSISTENT UNDERPERFORMANCE

If someone you manage is consistently a bottom performer and not getting better month over month, they have to go.

You see, your team is the wisdom and success of the crowd that you keep around them. If the crowd is incredibly smart, motivated, and hungry to win, that WIT mentality will spread like rapid-fire. But it takes only one consistently poor performer to slow down the team's progress.

When an outstanding team member sees an underperformer skating by, they'll think, "My leader doesn't care if I put in the work and accomplish the goal or not." This will cause them to slow down and get lazy, which will become a ripple effect on your team. So if you work really hard to coach up and help someone on your team, yet month after month they aren't improving or getting worse, they have to go.

#25
KILL BAD BEHAVIORS ASAP

The culture of any team is shaped by the worst behavior the leader is willing to tolerate.

Work to eliminate bad behavior immediately. If you can't get rid of the negative behaviors on the team, then the culprits of the worst behaviors may need to go next.

Bad behaviors lead to bad team members, and if bad team members spread like wildfire, this can destroy the culture and success of the team.

#26
CHANGE YOUR PERSPECTIVE ON TRADING TEAM MEMBERS

Managers are coaches building the best sports teams in the world. If you are a coach of a Super Bowl team and you have a team member who is negative, uncoachable, and not hard-working, then it's time to trade them.

I've worked with many managers, directors, and VPs who are scared to let go of team members who aren't a great fit. The key to coaching these managers is to understand that it's OK to trade underperforming employees to a different team.

Ultimately, the underperforming employee will be on a team or at an organization that better suits their needs and wants. And your team will be in a better situation overall.

When you have to let a bad employee go, instead of looking at it as firing them, think of it as trading them to a team where they're a better fit. Everybody wins with this mindset.

#27

IF YOU HAVE TROUBLE FINDING THE "RIGHT" TEAM MEMBERS, THE PROBLEM MAY BE YOU

This may be tough to hear or think about, but I know all-in leaders like you can handle the truth, so here goes. . .

If you go through rounds of hiring and firing, you might be the problem.

All-in leaders don't yell, put down, scream, cast judgment, or watch their employees' every move. All-in leaders are supportive and ask how they can help their team overcome their biggest challenges and problems. All-in leaders ask how they can help their team accomplish their greatest goals and desires. Instead of being upset that employees aren't exceeding expectations and are drowning in the day-to-day, teach them how to succeed and lend a helping hand.

Help your team get stuff done to succeed; otherwise, watch them churn and wonder why you can't find the right employees.

#28

BE PART OF THE SOLUTION, NOT THE PROBLEM

Great leaders don't yell and scream at their team. Great leaders don't try to watch their employees' every move. Great leaders are supportive and ask how they can help.

Instead of being mad, angry, or upset that employees are missing goals and drowning, roll up your sleeves and work on helping them get the water out of the sinking boat.

You are the leader. If the team is unsuccessful or is not hitting its goals, it's because of you. The buck stops with you.

#29

DURING STRESSFUL TIMES, RELEASE THE PRESSURE

When it's the end of the quarter and your team is scrambling to reach their goals, don't add fuel to the fire and make these stressful situations worse.

Great managers have a knack for releasing the pressure, putting everyone at ease, and decreasing the stress. When I say, "release the pressure," I don't mean taking on your employees' work. No one learns and grows in their position when you take on their workload for them.

When I say to "release the pressure," I mean provide a refreshing perspective. Instead of framing a project or a goal as "difficult," "impossible," or something that your team "has to do," frame these tasks as not only "possible" but "easy."

Mind over matter is key and shifting to this positive perspective will increase your team's productivity. More importantly, during high-stress situations, model for your team the type of upbeat, focused, and hardworking employee that they can be.

Not only will your employees have an example to look up to of what a top performer and a team player looks like, but you'll become the manager that everyone is trying to collaborate with.

#30

GET READY TO OVERCOME RESISTANCE WHEN YOU'RE MAKING WAVES

Creating long-lasting change offends people.

- When you are creating change, prepare to offend people.
- When you are creating change, prepare to upset people.
- When you are creating change, prepare to lose people.

When you are creating change, prepare to overcome hardship in the short-term to make essential movements for the long-term that help the company grow.

MONTH 8

EMPOWERMENT, TRUST, AND AUTONOMY

#1

WE'VE ALL BEEN UNQUALIFIED AT ONE POINT

I wasn't qualified to lead. . .until I led.

I wasn't qualified to speak. . .until I spoke.

I wasn't qualified to create. . .until I created.

The same is true for you.

Simply put, every single day, we are all unqualified to do a ton of things, but we get it done anyway. You may believe you aren't qualified to

- Lead that project (or that team)
- Speak at that meeting (or on that stage)
- Create that post (or that content)

What you'll start to find out is that you are more than qualified to do whatever it is you set your mind to.

So:

- Lead the project.
- Speak the words.
- Create the content.

The more you do, the more you'll become the all-in leader you always wanted to be.

#2

CREATE A BIGGER PURPOSE

People love working for all-in leaders for a number of reasons:

- Career advancement
- Personal growth
- A raise
- Less bureaucracy
- Greater impact
- A great boss
- Praise

But the real reason people love working for all-in leaders is that they create a sense of purpose for the team. So make it one of your major goals to create a purpose-driven environment for your team through your mission and vision.

#3

TEACH YOUR TEAM THE TRUE MEANING OF HAPPINESS

The million dollar question is, what is happiness?

Let me start by telling you what happiness isn't. If your definition or idea of happiness starts with the sentence "When I," you have the wrong idea.

I've been there. Trust me, that thing you thought will make you happy won't.

True happiness is the consistent persistent pursuit of maximizing your potential.

When you're in the consistent persistent pursuit of maximizing your potential, you are inspired. And when you're inspired to become the best that you can be, that is the true meaning of happiness.

#4

CRUSH ALL YOUR GOALS WITH THIS FRAMEWORK

SWTAR is an essential framework for crushing goals:

- Set a goal.
- Work on achieving it.
- Track progress.
- Achieve it.
- Repeat.

Enough said!

#5

ASK FOR INPUT

Maximize the trust within your team by asking your direct reports individually and collectively as a group for their input and ideas.

Increase the wisdom of the crowd by asking for strategies and recommendations to solve new challenges the team may face. Asking for input builds trust, appreciation, and a sense of security across the team.

#6

MAKE IT SAFE TO REACH OUT FOR HELP

If people on your team are stuck or need more information to accomplish a task, make sure you create an environment where asking for help or asking questions is safe.

I've worked for companies where the managers hated answering questions or helping when their team needed it. And I've worked for companies where they encouraged employees to ask for help.

The best leaders in the world know that they serve their team and their people. So, make a point to let everyone know that it's better to ask questions and ask for help than to stay stuck.

Be hungry to provide guidance to your team when they need it. This way nothing will ever slow your team down.

#7

ALWAYS ASK

Coach your people to ask because if you don't ask, the answer is always "no."

- Maybe it's a new project.
- Maybe it's a new idea.
- Maybe it's a department switch.
- Maybe it's a promotion.
- Maybe it's a big campaign or a new feature.

If you don't ask, the answer is always "no." So ask!

#8

THERE ARE TWO THINGS PEOPLE WANT MORE THAN MONEY AND POWER

People want recognition and praise.

Give recognition and praise early and often with new employees because the people who are constantly being built up are the people who achieve more. And the people who are constantly being torn down are the people who achieve less.

#9

HOST DAILY STANDUPS

Now that more companies are going remote and team members are rarely meeting face-to-face, a critical way to maximize team collaboration is to host daily standups. A *standup* is a quick 30-minute meeting where your entire team shares progress on goals.

For the standup agenda, have each team member highlight the following, round-robin style:

- **Key performance indicators (KPIs):** Regardless of whether the data is good or bad, share the progress you've made with KPIs.
- **Biggest wins:** These can be small wins or big wins. But each team member should celebrate their recent wins, whatever they are.
- **Biggest project updates:** What are the projects that team members are currently working on, and how is progress coming along on those projects?
- **Biggest opportunities for improvement:** What are some areas that need improvement?
- **Blockers:** What is holding you back from accomplishing your tasks and goals? Identify the blockers and work as a team to unblock them ASAP!

- **Priorities:** What priorities and tasks are team members going to work on for the day?

Provide praise or coaching to the team based on the data. Sincerely listen, take notes, and give your full attention.

#10
THE DATA DOESN'T LIE

Numbers never lie. They only provide you with the information you need to improve. Teach your team to track the important data metrics to manage their goals. If your people don't keep track, find a way to review numbers when needed.

By tracking the numbers daily, not only will your employees be better able to keep track of projects, but you can use the data to coach your team.

Here are some data-driven questions you can ask:

- How did you do compared to your goal?
- Are there opportunities for improvement?
- What did you learn from the A/B tests, and what would you change next time?

Collect the data, ask the right questions, take notes, and be ready to try again stronger and smarter next time!

#11
DITCH INTERNAL POLITICS

Coach your team to ditch internal gossip and politics.

You will never be criticized by someone who is doing more than you. You will always be criticized by someone doing less than you.

Never forget this, and ditch the politics.

#12
TEACH FAILURE

Many times you have to fall down to learn how to get back up and keep going.

To become an unstoppable team, everyone has to lose the fear of failure and be open to taking risks.

All-in leaders teach their team that it's OK to fail. The people you lead have to be willing to fail, or else they won't try new things that could move the team forward.

Try to be willing to fail forward as a leader and teach your team to take risks and fail forward as well because sometimes you have to get it wrong to learn how to get it right.

#13
UNBLOCK THE BLOCKERS

If there is any obstacle blocking your team's success, your job as a leader is to help them run over it, climb over it, dig below it, get around it, and do whatever it takes to get unblocked!

Teach your team that if they are ever blocked on a project, all they have to do is let you and their colleagues know right away in order to help.

Then do whatever it takes to tear down the obstacle and get unblocked right away.

#14

SEE THINGS THROUGH
TO THE END

Mediocre bosses and managers are great at coming up with amazing ideas that can potentially drive a ton of business, but they're terrible at seeing the project through to the end.

If you currently have or end up developing this mindset, you will have lots of half-finished projects on your hands.

Leaders who go all-in don't just have a knack for coming up with game-changing ideas, but they are the ultimate completionists. In fact, they are *obsessed* with seeing things through to the end and making sure the project gets completed.

Part of the reason why all-in managers are completionists is because they take full responsibility for their work from the very beginning. When you take 100% ownership for the outcome, you essentially put your reputation on the line and give yourself no choice but to launch and succeed.

With every project, the best managers raise the stakes so high, the only options are finish or bust. Even when bottleneck issues and problems come up, this doesn't discourage a leader.

They stay focused and keep their eye on the prize. Instead of doing the same things and expecting different results, when issues come up, all-in leaders create innovative ways to resolve the problem, change how work is handled at the company, and keep moving the ball forward.

By facing problems and rising to the occasion, great leaders show their team what going all out and doing whatever it takes looks like. Poor managers by contrast create a toxic culture of quitting when things get complicated.

They (unknowingly) teach their people to avoid obstacles at all cost and wait around for someone to hold your hand and help you. And if all else fails and no one can solve the issue, give up and move on to the next thing.

By contrast, the tenacious mentality of seeing things through to the end creates strong SWAT-style employees who jump in and do what they have to in order to resolve problems and fill in gaps. Then they jump back out and return to the usual responsibilities of their position.

There are so many benefits to toughing it out that if you want to be one of the world's best leaders, you have no choice but to develop a tenacious mentality and stick it out.

The bigger the obstacle, the more you have to leverage tunnel vision. Trust me. Seeing things through to the end pays off.

#15

BRING THEM IN TO GET BUY-IN

People buy into the process of your projects when you involve them.

If you work on a big or small project on your own in a vacuum for weeks or months and don't involve stakeholders, it will be harder to get their buy-in later on down the line. So, it's always best to get buy-in at the beginning.

If someone is onboarded and engaged in the decision-making process for a new idea, strategy, objective, or execution plan from the beginning, they will be excited and engaged to see it through to completion. Additionally, if you involve multiple stakeholders in the process, it lessens the load on your back.

So, bring the people you need into the projects you are working on early. Get buy-in and team-wide adoption and increase the chances of success.

#16

GET YOUR PEOPLE PUMPED ABOUT YOUR IDEAS

When you have a new idea or a new project and you want to get your people hyped and eager to crush it, you have to bring the energy!

Just presenting your idea in a boring, black-and-white slide deck with no excitement isn't going to cut it. Boring ideas are going to produce half-assed efforts and poor results. So, get creative with how you introduce your ideas because it's going to make the difference between a successful outcome and a bad outcome.

Pitch your idea like you're pitching a movie script to the greatest actors and producers in Hollywood. Tell a compelling story and take your team on the journey of how you came up with the idea.

- Why will this idea or project be valuable to your customers and the goals of the organization?
- Where will this project take the team and the entire organization?
- How will this idea or project be a game changer for the industry you work in?

Be passionate and dramatic in your delivery. The only way you're going to get your team pumped is if you yourself are pumped about your ideas.

#17

TURN YOUR WORDS INTO ACTIONS AND BUILD TRUST WITH YOUR EMPLOYEES

Becoming an all-in leader depends on the actions you take. However, the one crucial thing you need from your employees to be your best is trust.

A manager is nothing if their people have zero trust in them. All communication breaks down if there's no trust. Ultimately, the only way you're going to get your people to trust in you is through action.

If you talk about putting the employees first but your actions suggest that you're invested only in yourself, your people are going to pick up on that, not trust you, and produce poor results. But if you take actions that prioritize the advancement of your people, you're going to earn their trust and loyalty.

It's also important to point out that trust is never one-sided. You need to be able to trust your team, just as much as they trust you.

Here is how you can ensure that trust is a two-way street on your team:

- Train your people on all the rules they need to work independently without you standing over their shoulder, micromanaging them.
- With situations that are outside the rule book, take a step back and trust your people to make the best decisions based on the training you gave them and their own talents.
- Giving your employees the space and freedom to handle situations on their own only boosts their confidence and helps them grow.

#18

AUTONOMY TO CREATE
AND INNOVATE

Employees leave big companies when they become frustrated that their creative ideas aren't being implemented.

Many companies are good at performativity and asking for ideas on innovation. But then months go by, and they do absolutely nothing with those recommendations.

This is incredibly demoralizing and frustrating for people who have creative ideas and want to make a big splash at their company. Never forget that the people who work for you want to innovate. Don't stifle that creative flow for them.

No matter the size of your organization, work to create autonomy for your people to create and innovate. Simplify authorization processes as much as you can.

Keep your team efficient, autonomous, and free to create.

#19

THE 40-HOUR WORK WEEK IS A MYTH

Let's say you have an employee who is a total rock star. They produce quality work, and it doesn't take them long to crush their goals.

It's Thursday at the office, and by the time lunchtime rolls around, this rock-star employee has completed all the day's tasks. As a manager, what do you do?

A. Do you give them more work to do, so they're putting in their eight hours for the day?

Or. . .

B. Do you let them get off early?

If you answered "A," you're wrong. The correct answer is "B," and here's why: you don't want to be a micromanager.

Micromanagers think small. They would rather have an employee spend half the day playing around and take an entire eight-hour shift to complete their work than grind and complete the day's tasks in half the time.

I urge you to stop worrying about subjective rules like the 40-hour work week. If you have a rock star who is working smart, reward them for their hard work.

This is only going to motivate them to continue driving big results in the most time-efficient way.

#20
LEADERSHIP IS HARD

Leadership is not easy or glamorous. Leadership is all about giving to others with the expectation of nothing in return. Leadership is about never being too big to do any task at the company. Leadership is about genuinely caring about other people's success and growth more than your own. Leadership is about being the person who anyone can turn to when things get hard because they know you will find a way to help.

Be the best servant leader you can possibly be.

#21
SWEAT MORE IN PRACTICE, BLEED LESS IN WAR

To become the best they can be, teach your team to cut their teeth and make mistakes during practice rather than with clients and prospects.

The more you can become the best off the field, the more you will win on the field.

#22
BECOMING BETTER IS GREATER THAN BECOMING THE BEST

Train your team members that trying to become the best in the world is a costly mistake because it perpetuates the myth that you can be successful only by beating those around you.

Coaching your team to instead become better than who they were in the past shifts the focus from competing with others to competing with themselves and raising the bar.

Being better is always better than being the best.

#23

THE WORLD NEVER WANTS TO CHANGE...DO IT ANYWAY

This is the thing about changing the world: the world never wants to change. When you introduce a life-changing idea, product, or strategy to someone, more often than not, they're going to dig in their heels and resist.

Part of what makes all-in leaders great is that they aren't in the business of being popular. They're in the business of changing the world. If creating "change" causes people to want to hold you back and fight, then become someone who loves to win fights, because do you know who wins a fight? Whoever wants it more.

You were built for this. Who do you think wants it more? Them or you?

#24

TAKE A CIRCULAR APPROACH TO TEACHING

No matter what industry you work in, it's likely that your market is more competitive than ever before.

For companies to work their way to the top or maintain their dominance in their industry, you have to stay ahead of the trends. You have to keep reinventing your brand. Most importantly, you have to keep your customers excited about your brand, and the only way to do all this is to make teaching a priority.

When I say teaching, I don't just mean top-down teaching where you, as the manager, lecture with no feedback in return. When I say teaching, I mean taking a circular approach. You share your expertise, and your people, in turn, give you feedback on your teaching as well as their experiences with customers. (What works? What doesn't work? What do they need more of?)

When you and your people are teaching and learning from each other, this helps your team stay on top because it forces you to constantly adjust your coaching. It helps your team get on the leadership track by thinking beyond their position. And it helps you better understand and service your customers.

#25
LEARN FROM GOOD AND BAD EXPERIENCES

There are lessons you can learn from every single experience you have leading your team.

Some things you try to do with the team will go well. Other strategies you test will fail. Leaders who go all-in bounce back from failure with lessons learned to lead smarter next time, with no loss of enthusiasm. View every experience (failure or success) as a positive that taught you a valuable lesson.

Document the lessons learned and try again the second time around with even more passion.

#26

POSITIVITY IS POSSIBILITY

Just one small positive thought in the morning can change your whole day.

Work with your team to demand a positive can-do attitude. Every day, practice and preach positivity, coachability, hard work, and doing whatever it takes to serve the mission because positivity equals possibility.

Negative mindsets and actions kill more opportunities than anything else in the world.

- "I can't do it."
- "We won't do it."
- "I don't know how to do it."

None of that negativity will work. Abolish all negative thinking among your team and get everyone on board by being positive about the possibilities in the future.

A positive "can-do" attitude is the magic that helps teams become limitless.

#27

DITCH THE CRITICISM AND STICK TO POTENTIAL OPPORTUNITIES FOR IMPROVEMENT

Providing criticism to your team can be dangerous because it immediately puts employees on the defensive. Criticism can also foster resentment if an employee doesn't have the emotional intelligence and coachability to remain open-minded to your feedback.

Many psychological studies show that people respond better to positive reinforcement than negative. So instead of saying "Let me provide you with some criticism for improvement," don't.

No one likes to be criticized and told why they're doing something wrong. Instead, when you get the urge to criticize someone, stop and try to figure out why they do and say the things they do.

Take the moment to reflect rather than criticize because criticism never achieves a positive result.

#28
ALWAYS STAY TEACHABLE

From my 20 years of sales experience, I've learned that one of the biggest traps that managers fall into is complacency. And it's easy to understand.

When you've reached a certain level in your career, why continue to improve? You've made it! But if you want to become a better more dynamic team leader, you need to stay focused on staying teachable.

Think about the following:

- What results have you been producing lately?
- Have you shown improvement?
- Have you been staying the same or, worse, going backward?
- Have you been struggling to keep up with demands, goals, and quotas?

If there's a huge gap between where you are right now in your personal and professional life and where you want to be, this might be because you've become complacent and stopped being teachable.

To become one of those managers who make a positive impact with your employees, you have to learn to humble yourself and venture into areas where you're not an expert.

Be open-minded and be comfortable with being uncomfortable because when you're uncomfortable, that means you're learning and growing.

#29

EITHER YOU'RE MOVING FORWARD OR YOU'RE MOVING BACKWARD

In life, you're either moving forward or you're moving backward; the choice is yours. You can choose to stop growing and stay stuck. Or you can keep leveling up and moving forward. There's no in between.

Once you finish college, you have to go out on the market and get a full-time job. And once you get that full-time job, you have to work toward getting a promotion.

Every new level requires you to change. And at every new level there are going to be growing pains that you will have to overcome. But don't let new obstacles keep you from making progress.

If you have the drive to rise to the challenges of a new level, then there's nothing to be anxious about. Focus on your growth and you'll come out on the other side stronger.

#30

TODAY THE TEAM IS THE BEST IT'S EVER BEEN AND THE WORST IT WILL EVER BE

Teach your team this secret. It will teach them to never be content with success and the way things are. This secret will push them to constantly strive for better and realize that consistency (in effort, drive, work ethic, etc.) is the key to achieving your greatest dreams.

MONTH 9

LEADING THROUGH CHANGE, UNCERTAINTY, AND TOUGH TIMES

#1
CHANGE YOUR OUTLOOK ON FAILURE

Either you win or you learn. Either you crush it or you learn what you need to do next time to crush it. Failure is all about your outlook.

Instead of looking at failure as a negative, realize that failure is an opportunity to learn and improve.

There is no such thing as failure because if you learned a valuable lesson, then you haven't failed.

#2
EMBRACE CHALLENGES

As a manager, you're going to constantly come up against obstacles.

Things are going to go wrong more than they are going to go right. You're going to have projects where the work starts to pile up as you get closer to the deadline. You're going to accomplish major milestones, reach new peaks, and encounter new challenges you've never seen before.

But the difference between managers and all-in leaders is that a mediocre manager will see a challenge and be completely silent. They won't raise their hand and volunteer to tackle the challenge because they are looking at it in a negative light.

A challenge is going to mean tons of time, energy, and hard work. A challenge is an inconvenience to a mediocre manager.

It's a distraction that's going to cut into their paper pushing and productivity. Plus, what if the outcome is bad?

A mediocre manager will assume that a bad outcome will be a disaster for their career and their interest. But instead of looking at obstacles in a negative light, a true leader sees these issues as opportunities to become a better manager and help the company become unstoppable.

Instead of avoiding obstacles, embrace them.

#3
EMBRACE THE PAIN

Leading from the front lines is hard.

Leading anyone is hard.

Learning to become the best leader you can be is hard.

Motivating people to give 100% every day of the week is hard.

Doing things you've never done before and feeling like an imposter are hard.

Leading is never easy, so embrace the pain and rise up. Realize that every leader goes through hard times and painful experiences. You are not alone.

But anything worth doing is painful. Everyone who has led before you and anyone who will lead after you will have to do the same.

Embrace the pain and make it happen.

#4
YOU CAN ALWAYS IMPROVE

The most interesting part of leadership is realizing every single day just how little we know.

If you can embrace this reality, you will always be open to learning new strategies to improve as a manager and to improve the performance of your team.

#5

STOP PLAYING THE SHORT GAME

Coach your team to not give up on learning something, doing something, or mastering something when the going gets tough.

Anything you want to do is hard at first, so don't be too hard on yourself. Focus on becoming a 10-year success versus an overnight success and just keep going.

When you work at a new task that you've never done before, assume that during the first 20–48 hours, you will be terrible at it. But once you put in the work, you will learn and gradually get better over time.

#6

THERE'S STRENGTH IN CHANGE

Having the foresight and the wisdom to change directions is a superpower that requires a tremendous amount of insight and introspection.

New data equals new decisions. Don't be scared to change course. There's strength in change.

#7

GROWTH COMES FROM DISCOMFORT

Teach your team and yourself that growth comes from discomfort and hard work.

Growth requires every team member to leave something behind. This could be bad habits or beliefs. You will be uncomfortable letting go of your former life to make space for a new you in a new life.

This is why being prepared for discomfort in all phases of growth is important.

#8

ALL EMPLOYEES FALL INTO THESE TWO CATEGORIES

There are always two types of people on your team regardless of the industry you work in:

1. The person you give a task to and you still have to think about it or follow up to make sure it gets done.
2. The person you give a task to and you never have to worry about it getting done. They complete it at a level far greater than what you could have ever imagined.

Here's how to get the most value out of both types of employees:

- **Person #1:** Coach them up or out of the organization to become person #2.
- **Person #2:** Give them more recognition, pay, and promotion opportunities ASAP. This type of person is invaluable to the growth and success of your organization. Treat them like the gold that they are.

#9

MANAGE MEDIOCRE EFFORT WELL

Coach your people and remind them that they can't be upset by the results they didn't get with the work they didn't do.

To achieve the goals they want to achieve, they have to put in the hard work. Put in the work and crush your goals to get the results you want. . .or don't, and be angry when you fail to move the goalpost.

#10

MINDSET SAVES THE SINKING SHIP

Teach your team that ships don't sink because of the water around them. Ships sink because of the water that gets in them.

Coach your people to not let what's happening around them (the news, society, etc.) get inside their heads and weigh them down. Never let negative thoughts, current events, people, or criticism kill your success.

No water in the boat!

#11

PAY ATTENTION TO THE SUBTEXT

If you work remotely, always pay close attention to the subtext of your conversations with employees.

Pay attention to their tone in messages and their body language on Zoom calls. Also pay attention to their response times (email, Slack, etc.). If individuals become less responsive, there could be problems.

Be observant about the subtext and be ready to check in and assist with anything your employee may need if you notice any changes.

#12

FIND OUT YOUR TEAM'S WEAK SPOTS

It doesn't matter how smart, talented, and experienced you are. Crises are going to happen—it's inevitable.

Instead of running from this truth, the best managers prepare their teams by getting ahead of the crisis. Let's say your sales team's weak spot is follow-ups. They aren't following up with prospects at all, and then when the quarter is almost up, your team is scrambling to make quota because of this flaw.

A great manager will avoid this stress altogether by making note of the weakness early on, coaching the team on delivering value-driven follow-ups, and making it a requirement to follow up x number of times to drive the sales process.

Do the same for your team. Spot the weakness, provide whatever coaching and support your team needs, and avoid chaos later.

When you can stay calm and cool under pressure and take decisive action, your people will have greater faith and trust in you as the dynamic leader that you are.

#13

STEP OUTSIDE YOUR COMFORT ZONE

Whenever you decide to be complacent with the way things are, you cheat yourself.

As managers and leaders, there are so many things we should be doing more frequently in our personal and professional lives, from taking the time to recruit a few more hires to going outside and getting exercise. But we don't always do these things, because they're an inconvenience or they require us to go outside of our usual routines.

The more you decide to stay comfortable and stick to your routine, the more you cheat yourself out of becoming a better, healthier, happier, and more accomplished person.

Instead of constantly cheating yourself, I challenge you today to write down a professional life task (e.g. generate a few more leads, etc.) and a personal life task (e.g. read, spend time with your spouse, etc.) that you would like to complete. Then put in the effort to get those two goals completed.

#14
THERE'S NO ROOM FOR DRAMA

Gossip is common in lots of offices, but you don't have to tolerate it on your team.

Coach your employees to avoid negativity and refrain from participating in drama like gossiping because talking badly about someone else reflects poorly on the gossiper.

You should have zero tolerance for drama of any kind because team members who aren't focused on their goals don't have whatever it takes to achieve success.

#15

STOP MICROMANAGING

Think about the most tired or uninspired you've ever been at work.

It probably wasn't when you stayed late or when you came home from a long vacation. Chances are you were the most uninspired when you had someone looking over your shoulder and watching your every move.

This is what micromanagement is.

Micromanagement is the best way to kill innovation and happiness at work. Micromanagement involves hiring wonderful people and crushing their souls by telling them what to do every single hour of the day.

The most mentally fatigued people are those who feel they have no freedom to execute their jobs to the best of their ability. If you are the kind of leader who micromanages (be honest with yourself here), you may be afraid to loosen up the reins.

But the upside of eliminating micromanagement is that it allows the entire team to scale the efforts that make the greatest impact on the company's bottom line.

There is only one solution to micro management, and that is to trust. Trust that your people will perform and serve the company mission.

#16

YOU CAN DISAGREE, JUST DO IT WITH RESPECT

Teach your team that it's OK to disagree with a strategy or recommendation from their co-workers but to do it with kindness.

Everyone is entitled to their opinion, and we should respect each other's opinions. That doesn't mean you can be a jerk about it.

Be kind and polite. Appreciate their point of view. Share yours. Try to use the data from both sides to make the best decision possible.

#17

DON'T BE MEAN-SPIRITED OR DISRESPECTFUL (SERIOUSLY)

This secret is probably obvious, but I couldn't write a management secrets book without mentioning how important it is to be respectful and kind to every one of your employees at all times.

Don't ever raise your voice at someone. Don't ever call someone names or be insulting in any sense of the word. And don't ever curse at someone. Treat your people as you would want to be treated. It doesn't matter if they made a huge mistake or if you're stressed out and having a bad day.

There is no justifiable reason to be mean. Just like the saying goes, "You attract more flies with honey than vinegar," you'll get more out of your employees with kindness than aggression. So never take your anger out on your employees.

Being disrespectful creates a toxic culture where employees will mirror your behavior toward each other. There will be no team spirit, and you'll struggle through every goal.

Be respectful at all times. And if you can't do this, then re-consider your leadership position.

#18

TOUGH TIMES BUILD CHARACTER

The all-in leaders who stay positive and courageous in any negative situation always succeed.

Bad leaders fail when faced with negative situations by blaming others, acting out of fear, and being unkind to their team.

A smooth sea never made a skilled sailor. Tough times build great teams and leaders.

#19

RISE UP

You'll never be criticized by someone doing more than you. But you will always be criticized by someone doing less.

Teach the team to become immune to others' criticisms. Keep going and rise up.

#20

ASK YOURSELF THESE QUESTIONS BEFORE YOU MAKE A HUGE CHANGE

To keep going all-in with improving your team, sometimes you have to implement big changes, from expanding your team to taking on a new challenge or changing a policy.

Before you think about making a huge change, you should ask yourself the following questions:

- Is this the right time for this change?
- Does this change align with the company's goals?
- Will this change help make the team and/or the company better?
- Does your organization have the resources (finance, time, labor power, etc.) to make this change happen?
- Does this change have a clear course of action?
- Have you consulted other leaders at the organization and experts? Do they think this change is a good idea?
- Can this change be tested on a smaller level before doing a massive overhaul?

Once you go through these questions, if you find that you're answering "no" a lot more than "yes," then this change probably isn't a good idea right now for your team.

#21
MAKE DECISIONS WHEN YOU'RE ON TOP

Do you want to know the absolute worst time to make a decision? The worst time to make a decision is when you've made some mistakes, taken some losses, and now you're at a deficit.

If you can help it, you never want to make decisions when your team has been underperforming and missing their numbers because that desperation to make up for those failures ends up clouding your judgment. You're essentially so hungry for a solution that you will go for anything, even if it ends up being a poor solution that wastes time and money.

Instead, one of the best things you can do when you and your team are going through a rough patch is to keep your nose to the ground and grind it out.

Bad days don't last forever. If you encourage your team to keep putting their best effort forward, they will eventually score a huge win and be stronger because of the time they spent grinding.

Save the decision-making for the times when you and your team are on a roll with the wins because you aren't desperate to get out of the hole.

You're thinking ahead to your next win, so your judgment is crystal clear.

#22

YOUR TEAM'S IDEAS HAVE THE POTENTIAL TO CHANGE THE WORLD

Your team's ideas can be innovative and transformative. Too often, however, great ideas from the team are never shared because of two reasons:

- Fear
- Perfection

Fear keeps a lot of people from sharing their ideas with the team. But it's not about perfection; it's about progress.

Coach your team to overcome fear and perfection. Coach your team that any idea they have, big or small, can change the world, so they should share it.

Even if it doesn't get acted on right away, that one idea can be a positive domino effect and the beginnings of something that could change the world.

Always take progress over perfection and fear.

#23

GET IN THE TRENCHES WITH YOUR TEAM

When I was selling for IBM, the one thing I hated was my management always telling me what I needed to do but never leading by example.

They would always say:

"You need more appointments."

"You need more sales."

"Why hasn't this deal closed yet?"

I would ask for help with prospecting or closing, and they always scoffed at me and told me to figure it out. When I finally started to lead teams, I told myself I would never lead like that from the top of the ivory tower.

- If you are in sales, get in the trenches with your team and lead from the front lines.
- If you are in marketing, get in the trenches with your team and write ads, post social content, and help identify the needs and pains of the audience.
- If you are in product or engineering, help code or strategize the architecture of the next big feature.
- If you are in HR, help recruit top talent.

Always lead from the trenches.

People appreciate all-in leaders who roll up their sleeves, get their hands dirty, and put in the work.

#24
ASK MORE QUESTIONS

The greatest leaders I know always seem to have no fear of looking stupid.

Whenever they didn't know something, they would just ask. And it's amazing what happens when you ask a question.

If you don't understand or know something, get over your pride and just ask.

#25
STUDY FEEDBACK PATTERNS

When you study the feedback you are getting from people who work for you, you will start to see a series of patterns (good or bad).

If several people on your team are telling you the same thing, there is probably some truth to it. You can leverage these patterns to multiply great results or minimize poor performance.

Don't resist change to improve the feedback patterns. Whenever you feel the urge to resist, you have to ask yourself this:

"Would you rather be right, or would you rather be successful?"

What feedback have you been getting from your team, company, co-workers, clients, boss, etc. that you need to pay more attention to and take action on?

#26

LEAD WITH EMPATHY WHEN CHALLENGES ARISE

When someone on your team misses a deadline or generates subpar work, do you berate them and punish them?

Or do you ask questions to find out if there's an underlying issue that's causing the problem?

I remember that right before my mom died of Alzheimer's, I had to rush to see her. The timing was terrible. It was three days before a demo day when I needed to fundraise venture capital or my company would die.

That week I missed deadlines because my mind was focused on my mom. My team could have easily criticized me for not bringing my A game. They could have yelled and beaten me down before asking what was going on. However, that isn't how we lead teams here at Seamless.AI.

At Seamless.AI, everyone knows that if there is any underperformance, we lead with empathy and try to figure out the root issue.

When you lead with empathy, you don't want to beat down someone already struggling. Instead, you want to figure out what's holding them down so you can help them move forward.

#27

THIS GETS IN THE WAY OF TAKING RESPONSIBILITY

If taking responsibility for your life were easy, everyone would do it.

So, why is it so hard to take 100% ownership? Taking complete ownership (especially during the bad times) can be so difficult because change is one of the biggest hurdles to jump over.

When you're on a success journey, it's always easier to complain than to change your behavior. Change is uncomfortable.

It takes discipline, effort, and intentionally stepping outside of your comfort zone.

Ultimately, most people would rather be comfortable than uncomfortable. But if you want to learn how to become a true leader and how to take responsibility and absorb the blows for your team, you have to learn how to embrace change.

#28
TEACH THE DEFINITION OF FAILURE

Failure isn't missing the target. Failure is never taking the shot in the first place.

Teach your team the definition of failure and to always take the shot. If they miss, fail forward and shoot again.

Failure is a learning opportunity that helps you operate smarter next time. Failure gives you the data to try again smarter and faster.

Keep shooting. And don't be discouraged by failure.

#29
HELP YOUR TEAM GET UNSTUCK

When your people are struggling with a negative mindset, one strategy to help them is to share motivational, positive videos and quotes. I've seen people's entire mood shift from a few inspiring words.

Every day I post a motivational quote and video to our entire company because we all get stuck in the daily grind of our day-to-day lives, and sometimes we need to take a step back and reflect on a positive message. Motivational videos and quotes help.

Share a motivational video or quote with your team today to help them get unstuck.

#30

REMIND YOUR PEOPLE HOW UNSTOPPABLE THEY ARE

So many people on your team will tell themselves that they are not worthy of getting that promotion. Teach your people that they are more than qualified.

When I built my third company, the smartest venture capitalists in the world said I wasn't qualified to build Seamless.AI.

Today Seamless.AI is thriving because I didn't listen to them and what they thought I was qualified or not qualified for. Imagine how successful you and your team would be if they believed they were good enough to make anything happen. This is how leaders build unstoppable teams.

Coach your team so they have all the skills and talent they need to make it happen and take action today.

#31

HAVE RELENTLESS OPTIMISM

You and your team have to exude relentless optimism at all times.

Being optimistic, focusing on solutions, and having a positive outlook are 90% of the battle when leading and managing top-performing teams. Whether the team is exceeding targets or not, be optimistic.

Whether the business is going through a winning season or a losing season, be optimistic.

- If you are ahead or behind goals, be optimistic.
- If you are happy or sad, be optimistic.
- If you are having a good day or a bad day, be optimistic.
- If the economy is skyrocketing or crashing, be optimistic.

When there is a will, there is always a way. It's always possible to find a solution to a problem if you think it's possible. Conquer the hard truths, the tough times, and the brutal facts with relentless optimism.

It's one of the keys to successful leadership. Use it daily and teach your team to walk the walk of relentless optimism daily.

PART IV

THE SECRETS TO DEVELOPING
THE NEXT GENERATION
OF LEADERS

MONTH 10

THE HUMAN ELEMENT, EMOTIONAL INTELLIGENCE, AND SOFT SKILLS

#1

RECOGNIZE THE DIFFERENCE BETWEEN BAD BOSSES AND ALL-IN LEADERS

As you continue to hone your leadership skills, your ultimate goal shouldn't be to become the best manager. Your goal should be to become the best leader.

Leaders inspire their team to dream big, do more, be more, and accomplish things that they didn't think were even possible.

When you wake up every day, your goal should be to maximize the performance and overall happiness of your team.

This is the mission of a great leader.

Act. Do. Believe. Become.

#2

EMBRACE THE GREATEST CHANGE WHEN YOU BECOME A LEADER

When you become a leader, it's not about your success anymore. Your individual contributions no longer matter.

The only thing that matters as a leader—your only goal as a leader—is to help each individual on your team become more successful. Your only goal is to help every single person on your team maximize their success.

Measure each person's results. Every day, do whatever it takes to help your employees expand their impact.

#3

TO HONE YOUR INTUITION, YOU HAVE TO FOCUS ON YOUR STRENGTHS

Some of the world's greatest leaders have a nearly impeccable sense of intuition. When you have great intuition, you don't need to wait for a minor problem to become a hurricane of an issue in order to do something.

Great intuition helps you see the underlying issues that others cannot see.

When your intuition is operating at its greatest potential, it becomes the foundation of dynamic decision-making because a great intuition will help you figure out the top priorities now, spot issues well before they happen, and identify opportunities.

There's a misconception that intuition is something either you have or you don't. And while intuition is an integral part of impactful leadership, it's more than just instincts.

Intuition is a natural instinct, but it's also a skill that you have to practice. Intuition, like anything else, can and will improve if you diligently work to strengthen it.

While some leaders have a great, natural instinct, if you know intuition is your weak area, you are not a lost cause! Hone your instincts by getting to know yourself better.

Learn your strengths and your weaknesses because, typically, the areas you're really strong in are also areas that you have a natural ability for. These strengths are the foundation for a rock-solid intuition.

Do an inventory of your strengths and your flaws, and work on honing your intuition in those strong areas.

With this secret, you'll be able to carry out more intuitive leadership.

#4
NEVER CALL ME YOUR "BOSS"

Train your team to never call you their boss.

I remember when I was in a meeting with the team and someone said, "Thank you, boss!" I appreciated the respect, but I told them, "Please don't ever call me your 'boss.' I'm your business partner." I said this because I don't believe in being a "boss."

A great leader is someone who is there to inspire you to achieve more, not depend on you to feed their ego with trivial monikers like "boss."

Anyone who demands that you call them a boss is a bad leader.

Don't cave to your ego like that.

#5
STAY TRUE TO YOURSELF

Authenticity is key to effective communication. Authenticity doesn't just mean honesty. It also means being true to who you are.

Just because you're in a leadership position doesn't mean you have to change who you are and start talking like a corporate robot. You also don't have to go out of your way to try to sound profound and eloquent 24/7.

People are the most receptive to sincerity, and they will respect authenticity. So, bring your unique voice and perspective to all your communication.

#6
ASK OPEN-ENDED QUESTIONS

If you want to understand your employees more, ask open-ended questions.

"Yes" or "no" questions won't give you much insight or help you get to know your employees better. But questions like "Tell me more" and "What do you think about X?" will elicit more expansive and thoughtful answers.

Further, instead of immediately responding after an employee gives an answer, pause. It may feel a little awkward at first, but it's a great interview tactic to get the other person to elaborate.

If you want to learn more about your team, ask an open-ended question.

#7
NEVER BE SATISFIED WITH THE STATUS QUO

Remind your employees of all they've accomplished thus far and get them excited about the progress they've made.

Never be satisfied with the results and progress of the status quo, because there's so much more to accomplish.

We can always improve.

We can always learn.

We can always work to optimize.

Recognize that your potential and the potential of the entire team are far greater than you or anyone even sees.

Set big goals, and go all-in to achieve them. Coach your team to be happy with everything they have done to be exactly where you are today.

Also coach your team to never be satisfied with the status quo. There is so much more potential in them to change the world, serve others, and make a positive impact.

#8

FIND OUT YOUR EMPLOYEES' COMMUNICATION STYLE

The best way to figure out your team members' communication styles is to simply ask.

Ask your people about their communication preferences.

- Some people prefer in-person conversations.
- Some people prefer texts.
- Some people prefer step-by-step guidance and frequent check-ins.
- Some people prefer to have the space to work on their own terms.

Everyone's communication style is different, and there's no one-size-fits-all approach. Instead of trying to guess, just come right out and ask; then adjust your style to fit every individual.

#9

STOP WORRYING ABOUT WHO'S RIGHT

Bad leaders care about who's right. Great leaders care about what's right.

#10
SHOW COMPASSION THROUGH ACTION

A lot of companies (especially startups) think that a one-for-all, team culture is all about the superficial.

In other words, a lot of startups think that that if they have "cool," materialistic stuff like bean bag chairs or free iPads that somehow these trivial things will communicate to their employees that, unlike a traditional office setting, they genuinely care about their people. However, reducing your culture to the superficial is insulting to your employees.

This barely scratches the surface as far as the true impact your organization can make on employees. If you really want to develop a "whatever it takes" culture where your employees feel that they are more than a filled seat and that leadership genuinely cares about them, you have to show your compassion through action and policy change.

Have one-on-ones with each of your employees and conduct anonymous surveys where you find out what your people want to see from the organization.

Make policy changes (benefits, paid vacation time, mental health, etc.) that reflect the feedback you receive from your people.

These are the actions that show not only that you care about your employees but that you take their opinions seriously and cherish their loyalty to the company.

#11
DON'T BE A KNOW-IT-ALL

No one wants to work with know-it-all managers because they zap all the creative energy in the room and try to make everything about them and what they know instead of pushing the task at hand forward.

Having a know-it-all mindset is the kiss of death for any manager with potential. Once you start to let your ego take over, you become complacent with your knowledge and experience, and you don't strive to learn more or to grow.

When you start thinking that you know everything, you lose everything. And you end up taking several steps back, mentally and emotionally.

The best leaders know that life is about constant elevation because there is no such thing as perfection and knowing everything. The best leaders know that no matter how big they get, they're never too big for great advice from anyone. So take good advice wherever you can get it.

Despite your leadership position, remember that growth and development never stop. After all, success is a marathon, not a sprint.

And the know-it-alls lose before they even get started.

#12

IT'S TIME FOR LEADERS TO GIVE A DAMN

It is more important now than ever to seriously care about your employees.

Don't claim to have culture and claim to put your people first and then do nothing to ensure that your employees have full, well-rounded lives.

Talk to your employees. Actually listen to them. Figure out what their passions are and what motivates them. Then act on the information you're given.

Listening and taking action show that you care.

#13

MAKE INTUITION AND DATA YOUR ULTIMATE DRIVERS

Let intuition drive testing. Let data drive decision-making.

#14

UNLOCK YOUR EMPLOYEES' NATURAL TALENTS

If you want to fully maximize your employees' abilities and potential, you have to be open-minded, because talent can come in many different forms.

Don't stick to the one cookie-cutter ideal you have in your mind about what a promising candidate in any given role should look like. Look beyond organizational charts if you want to spot diamonds in the rough.

Pay attention to the things your employees excel at naturally without any training. Then pinpoint the hidden talents that are there and the skills that enable them to thrive at this task.

Brainstorm different roles, projects, and opportunities for the employees to leverage those abilities. Then when the employee succeeds, give them a shout-out to encourage others to follow suit.

Your people will be excited to take on these new challenges, happy that their talents are being acknowledged, and you get to leverage your team to their fullest potential.

Sometimes leveraging employees' hidden talents will lead to resignations where they decide to change paths and take that gift elsewhere, but even when that happens, celebrate the new journey they're taking!

They'll be grateful for the opportunities you gave them and refer you and your company to others.

#15

TEACH YOUR TEAM MENTAL HEALTH RESILIENCE

A bad day, a bad week, or a bad month doesn't mean it's over.

Throughout your life, no matter what you do or who you work for, you will have difficult times. But it's important to focus on optimizing your mental health.

Take some time today to unplug, disconnect, and recharge so you have the energy to conquer your challenges.

Remember that every day is a new day filled with massive opportunities.

#16

REMEMBER, YOUR EMPLOYEES COULD BE ANYWHERE ELSE

The worst managers think that their employees should be grateful that they have a job. Instead of feeling like your employees should be grateful for their job, you should feel grateful that you get to lead them as their manager.

Your employees could work at a thousand other companies, but they chose to work with you. Never forget that.

If you operate every day with this mindset, you'll be a better leader and more effective manager, and you'll be more perceptive of your employees' needs and wants.

If you acknowledge that an employee can be working for someone else, when they make mistakes, fail, or underperform, instead of looking to point the finger (which leads to nothing), you try to figure out what the underlying issue is.

- Do they need some kind of support?
- Are they going through something in their personal life?

When you remember that your people could be anywhere else, it keeps you humble and makes you a compassionate leader that your employees will never forget.

#17

ENCOURAGE A WORK–LIFE BALANCE

Work–life balance is imperative to avoiding burnout.

Here are different actions you can take to help your people achieve a work–life balance that fits their needs:

- **Achieve your own work–life balance:** You can't expect your people to achieve a more balanced lifestyle if it's clear to everyone that you're constantly exhausted and grinding 24/7. So, do what you have to do to set an example for your team. Taking care of yourself will make you a better leader and show your people what a productive, balanced employee looks like.

- **Do check-ins with your employees:** In your one-on-ones, sincerely ask your employees how they are doing mentally and emotionally. What do they need from you to achieve greater work–life balance?
- **Encourage self-care:** During stand-ups and one-on-ones, talk about work–life balance and discuss different ways your people can practice self-care. Encourage them to take short breaks throughout the day. Go outside and get fresh air. Enjoy their favorite hobbies on the weekends.
- **Do regular follow-ups:** Check in and see how employees are managing their work rather than getting overwhelmed by their schedule. Are they exhausted trying to keep up or is their workload do able? This will help you get a better sense of what a realistic timeframe looks like for certain tasks.
- **Encourage quarterly paid time off:** Encourage your employees to take time off at the end of every quarter. And when they do take off, do not text, call, or email them. Let them truly take off without any work interruptions. Encourage your people to work hard but also rest up so they can play hard.

#18
PEOPLE DON'T CHOOSE A JOB, THEY CHOOSE A BOSS

The best bosses support people's growth and future. These leaders are invaluable to everyone who works for them.

Become an invaluable leader.

Inspire people's future potential.

Help people grow to become who they are meant to be.

And believe they can achieve more than what they even think they can achieve.

#19
TREAT YOUR PEOPLE LIKE FAMILY, NOT QUOTAS

When you treat someone like a quota or a cog wheel in a factory, they will fundamentally know that you don't care about them. But if you treat your team like family, they will care more and produce far greater results.

People don't care how much you know until they know how much you care. When you treat people who work for you like family, they know you care about them, and that is the difference between a mediocre leader and a great one.

#20
LOOK TO SHARED EXPERIENCES TO BUILD RELATIONSHIPS

At the root of great management and leadership are the relationships you build with your employees.

You want to build genuine connections with your people. To do that, you have to go above and beyond the superficial stuff like figuring out their learning style and their likes and dislikes.

To get past the superficial, set up dinners, work trips, etc.—anything where you get the chance to spend time with your people outside of the office.

These experiences are great opportunities to build camaraderie, grow relationships, and make memories with your employees, which are the key ingredients to lasting, genuine connections.

Because Seamless.AI is completely remote, these are rare opportunities for me, so I make a point a couple times every year to fly out leaders from the company to Florida, where we strategize, workshop, and, of course, do vacation activities (jet skis, etc.).

As a leader, these are some of the moments I cherish the most because not only do they give me the chance to optimize Seamless.AI at the micro level and work hands-on with my leadership, but I also get to know everyone better.

While you don't have to do anything as big as hosting a getaway mastermind, make it a habit to seize those moments outside of the office where you can make memories with your team and build that connection.

#21
STAND UP, STAND OUT

I wanted to share this leadership secret after I had to stand up for one of our customer success (CS) employees who was getting berated by a rude customer. This customer couldn't log in to our software because they couldn't figure out how to reset their password, and they opted to take their frustrations out on my CS manager.

My CS manager came to me with the issue, and I jumped on the phone and asked the customer politely not to disrespect our team who is working hard to serve them. All the customer had to do was check their email and reset their password!

When the customer realized how minor the issue was, they apologized for treating our team poorly and everyone won. The customer got what they wanted, and my CS manager was grateful that I had their back. This moment reminded me that the greatest leaders I've ever worked for always went all-in to stand up for their people, instead of cowering to unruly clients.

Always stand up for your people, especially when they are experiencing their greatest challenges.

#22

PUT YOURSELF IN YOUR BOSS' SHOES

Going all-in doesn't just mean being hyper-aware of company priorities or handling only what's asked of you. You have to have a knack for figuring out the issues your higher-ups are focused on.

Instead of writing their higher-ups off as difficult to work with and impossible to please, dynamic leaders stop working in the dark and find out the unsolved problems, the unaccomplished goals, and the pain points that their bosses are concerned about.

Great leaders then make these issues a top priority. If you're not sure what your boss' or your higher-ups' priorities are, be observant and pay attention to the issues they keep circling back to in meetings and conversations. And think about how you can contribute your expertise and your strengths to this issue.

Make a point today to stop thinking about the ways that your boss could be better, and put yourself in their shoes.

Doing this will only strengthen your professional relationship with your boss and strengthen your impact on the organization.

#23

"I'M JUST BEING HONEST" DOESN'T GIVE YOU A LICENSE TO BE A JERK

"I'm just being honest" is a terrible excuse to be rude and unkind to your people.

Many leaders will use the "I'm just being honest" line as a reason to be impolite or hurtful. But transparent leadership is all about being forthcoming in what you have to say and doing it with care and kindness.

Always be respectful in how you deliver constructive feedback. Remember, it's OK to be direct with your people; just be considerate and empathetic with how you deliver feedback for improvement.

#24
EMBRACE WHAT SETS YOU APART

As you add new individual contributors to your team, many will have doubts about their abilities. Teach all your individual contributors that their difference is their advantage.

People come from all walks of life with unique experiences, successes, and failures. By teaching the team that their difference is their advantage, they will share their perspective, their journey, and their life lessons to help the entire team level up.

Your team's differences are the ultimate advantages you will have at your discretion to win in the game of business.

#25
BE FULLY PRESENT AT MEETINGS

Bad leaders multitask, don't listen, have no agenda, and are all over the place during team meetings.

Great leaders are focused, have a tight agenda, listen to their team, take notes, develop an action plan after the meeting, and ensure that summaries of meetings are shared. If you are going to take the time to meet with your team, then make the time worthwhile by being present.

How you show up is everything.

#26

ALWAYS EXUDE HIGH EMOTIONAL INTELLIGENCE

Control of your mind, emotions, and actions is a strength.

Your ability to remain calm under pressure requires mastery. Work to get to a point in all facets of your personal life and professional life where your mood doesn't shift based on the insignificant actions of someone else.

Don't allow your emotions or the emotions of others to cloud your emotional intelligence. Don't allow others to control the direction of your team or the direction of your life. When you find yourself under extreme circumstances, remain calm, cool, and collected.

You and your team have got this.

#27

NEVER MAKE YOUR EMPLOYEES FEEL DUMB

Every employee wants to feel important, appreciated, and respected. The people who work for you like to feel capable and competent in their day-to-day work.

It doesn't matter how great the company or the product is, if you make your people feel stupid, you will fail as a manager, and your team will eventually fail and live up to the criticism that you dole out.

If a leader makes an employee feel stupid, they will start to disengage emotionally and eventually quit. Instead of being negative and making your people feel worthless, make your people feel valued. When they make mistakes, don't attack them over it. Be positive and turn mistakes into learning lessons. Coach them up.

You always want to take your people up to the top with you, rather than putting people down.

#28

WHEN YOU CARE LESS ABOUT YOUR PEOPLE, YOUR PEOPLE BECOME CARELESS

When you care more about your people, your people care more, too. The more I care and do for the people I lead, the more results and impact I see in return.

The choice is yours.

#29

DO WHAT YOU SAY AND SAY WHAT YOU DO

One of the greatest qualities of a great leader is building trust with your team. One of the keys to building trust with your team is doing what you say you are going to do.

Communication and action to support the team build trust. Do what you say and say what you do.

#30

LET SOMEONE KNOW YOU'RE PROUD OF THEM

You can get so caught up in the day-to-day grind and hustle of execution plans that it can be easy to forget to say these five powerful words to your team members: "I am proud of you."

If you go to work every day demanding more out of your people without letting them know how much you appreciate them, they will eventually leave you for a leader and a company that does.

Don't assume that showing your appreciation has to be a task. It takes only a few seconds to reach out to someone on the team who is working hard or consistently showing up no matter what and letting them know: "I am proud of you."

Who have you told this to lately? Who haven't you told this to lately? It takes two seconds to reach out.

Make a list of people who need to hear this and let them know today how much you appreciate them.

MONTH 11

LEADING DIVERSE TEAMS AND FOSTERING CONTINUOUS LEARNING

#1

DON'T LET DIFFERENCES KEEP YOU FROM GOLD

For every organization out there, big or small, whenever you put lots of people with different backgrounds, different experiences, and different personalities together and ask them to work toward a common goal, there are going to be clashes.

You, as the manager, are not going to be compatible with every person on your team, and that is OK. In fact, it's an unavoidable reality.

While you may not be compatible with everyone, as the manager, you are expected to put your differences aside, produce maximum results for the company, and win together. If you're (knowingly or unknowingly) disregarding someone on your team just because you don't like them, the joke is on you.

You're the one who's failing as a leader and potentially missing out on that person's ideas, insights, and maximum talents. Don't throw out great ideas and feedback because you don't like the source where it's coming from.

More importantly, don't let something as trivial as a personality clash keep you from being the best leader you can be. Approach every relationship you have on your team with optimism, and evaluate every idea objectively, with an open mind.

Mentor everyone equally and guide all of your people to their best selves, whether you get along with them or not.

#2
LEARN TO LEAD

I hope you know and believe this wholeheartedly by now, but it's critical for you to become the best leader in the world—not just so you can build the life you always wanted but for all the people who follow you, so they can learn from you and build the career they've always wanted.

If you help enough people get everything they want in life, you can have it all, too.

Work hard on becoming the best leader you can be every day. And learn to lead not for you but for all of those who follow you.

#3
RECOGNIZE WHEN YOU'RE AT THE TOP OF YOUR LEADERSHIP GAME

You know you're at the top of your leadership game when you wake up every day to go to work and you never feel like you're managing. You are waking up every day on a mission to help your employees win.

The job of a leader is to unlock the greatness of every single person on the team.

The job of a leader is to help inspire, support, teach, defend, and lift up every person to the highest levels of success.

#4

YOUR REPUTATION IS EVERYTHING

An all-in leader's job is to give to the team, not take from them.

Make it a goal to build a reputation company wide as a servant leader. Be generous with your time and energy to help your team succeed.

Help your team members reach their next goal, lead with empathy, and be authentic and selfless with your work. Take gutsy action that helps elevate the company, and deliver genuine wisdom.

If you consistently execute these servant leadership principles, you will earn the respect of your team and carve out the best reputation as a leader.

#5

SHARE YOUR NUMBER-ONE GOAL AS A LEADER

Companies often hire managers who either don't care about their employees or don't know how to maximize their success.

So when you are in team meetings, reinforce trust with your team and make sure to share that your number-one goal is to maximize their success. It's a small gesture, but it helps boost morale and improve your relationship with your people. When employees know that you're not "out to get them," they start looking at you as a mentor, and they take their walls down.

Once you make this clear to your team, do whatever it takes to actually deliver on that promise to unlock their potential and maximize their success.

#6

GO ABOVE AND BEYOND

Coach the team on one critical sign of a great employee: they should do something important that moves the business forward even if they weren't asked to do it.

Coach your employees to be self-starters and work on the projects that are going to produce the biggest returns without you having to hold their hand every step of the way.

#7

ALWAYS HAVE FIVE MINUTES FOR YOUR TEAM

Always be available for a quick five-minute call.

I don't care how busy I am. I will never be too busy for a five-minute call with someone on my team who needs me. Whether it's a quick question, a strategic idea for growth, or a quick sync, I'm here.

Why?

Because no matter how busy a great leader is, they take the time to help their people when they need it.

Always be available to support your troops.

#8

FIGURE OUT WHAT YOUR TEAM NEEDS AND HOW YOU CAN HELP

Today I want you to think about this question:

"What does the team need today, and what can I do about it?"

When I ask this question, I think about:

- What can I help get the team?
- What can I buy the team to help them hit their goals?
- What can I help coach the team on?
- What playbooks can I help create or improve?

Always ask yourself, "What does the team need, and what can I do to help?" because when you help your team win, you win.

#9

CUSTOMIZE YOUR ONE-ON-ONES

While we provided templates to help you maximize the success of the individual contributors on your team, be sure to customize for each person.

Some individual contributors will need coaching on strategy, execution, and the day-to-day tasks, while others will need coaching on mindset, health, and habits.

Some will need coaching on communication and time management, while others may need coaching on skill gaps to maximize their success.

Whatever the employee needs, make sure your coaching plans are highly customized to the strengths and weaknesses of every person on your team.

At the end of the day, you don't want to force a round peg into a square hole and push coaching on an employee that's irrelevant to their needs.

#10
GET YOUR PEOPLE SOLD ON THE PRODUCT AND THE COMPANY

If your organization is trying to build their client base, keep in mind that clients won't care about your company if your employees don't care.

It's crucial that you get your employees sold on the product because an employee who genuinely believes in the life-transforming potential of their product will sell it with passion and won't be disgruntled by any obstacles along the way.

To get your employees to bring the passion, try these strategies and get them sold on your product and company:

- **Educate your people on the product:** Make sure your employees are experts on the product and the company. How did the product come about? What needs does the product address? How is your solution different from competitors? Your employees should know everything about the product and company history because knowledge unlocks passion.
- **Share case studies:** Regularly share clients' success stories. When you show your people how your product is making clients' lives better, they are going to do everything they can to get it in everyone's hands.
- **Share employee testimonials:** Share the success stories of other employees. Maybe you have employees who've achieved major milestones like buying their dream home because of your company. These stories show contributors that they can accomplish anything at an outstanding organization like yours.
- **Give your people a stake in the product:** People always work harder when they feel they have some ownership in the product.

Give your employees opportunities through anonymous surveys and bi-weekly one-on-ones to share insight on how the product and the company can improve. Then actually implement the strongest ideas.

#11

INVEST YOUR RESOURCES TO MAXIMIZE EMPLOYEES' SUCCESS

So many people think that if you invest a ton of money into an employee and that person leaves, you lose that money you invested. But that thinking is wrong.

I had an intern, Nathan, who worked for my company while he was still in college. I made a point to support Nathan in his professional development through training and mentorship because I knew he had the potential to be a top performer, and he actually lived up to my expectations. Nathan crushed it while he worked for me.

Unfortunately (for me at least), when he graduated, Dell EMC came to him with an offer he couldn't refuse.

Although I was sad to see him go, I was ecstatic about his success. Fast-forward a few years later, and I'm hyper-scaling my business from 5 people to 500 people. Well, Nathan ends up referring a ton of people to come work at the company, who end up being some of my best performers, because Nathan never forgot the investment I put toward his professional development.

If you invest your time, money, and effort into someone, guess what's going to happen? Not only will they perform their best, but if they ever leave, they will never forget your support and pay you back tenfold.

The manager who invests the most in their people will always win.

#12

NIP YOUR INSECURITIES IN THE BUD

The best leaders put the needs of the team above everything else. But making your team your number-one focus is easier said than done because it's in our nature as humans to be self-centered.

When things go wrong, our instinct is to protect our interests and point the finger. And when things go right, our instinct is to take center stage and receive all the credit. This is why when you're managing your team, you have to learn to curb those impulses and do occasional check-ins with yourself.

If you're finding some lingering insecurities, nip them in the bud because those doubts are going to make it impossible for you to maximize your potential as a leader and empower your team.

If you're constantly looking for a pat on the back because you have deep-seated insecurities about your abilities, you aren't going to be able to help your people become the best versions of themselves.

So do a check-in with yourself. Make sure you are confident in your abilities, talents, and unique importance to the organization so that you can lead your team to greatness.

#13

OVERCOME IMPOSTER SYNDROME

Wherever you are on your journey to success, you are a few steps ahead of someone else. You are great, and you are meant to lead. Too many leaders with incredible experiences, intelligence, and purpose allow fear to hold them back from being the best.

You are an expert to someone. A role model to someone. A leader to someone.

Ditch the self-doubt and the imposter syndrome because you are right where you belong. And don't let anyone (including yourself) tell you otherwise.

#14

DON'T BE TOO HARD ON YOURSELF

Becoming a great leader requires hard work, and it doesn't happen overnight.

You will have some very challenging days, and sometimes you may even have doubts about your ability to lead others. My best advice to you is to be gentle with yourself. Don't be too hard on yourself; this is just a natural part of the process.

Never lose hope, hold on to your faith, and continue developing as a leader because every improvement you make brings you one step closer to becoming the best leader you can be.

#15

YOU ARE LIMITLESS

Inspire and motivate your team to believe in something beyond their own limited thinking.

#16

LIVE WITH AN ABUNDANCE MINDSET

Have you ever noticed the happiest people always seem to be doing something for others?

They see potential everywhere and in everyone, including themselves. What ties most of these people together is an abundance mindset. It's a belief that they'll do well in their life on their own merits and even better by bringing people up and along with them.

You often see that abundance mindset on LinkedIn where lots of experts share their hard-earned knowledge, instead of gatekeeping it. And we all benefit as a result.

So, what can you do today to live with an abundance mindset?

Take some time today to share something you're knowledgeable about with someone trying to learn it. So if you're a senior customer success manager, for instance, give insight into your playbook with a junior rep. If you're an account executive, show that struggling sales rep a few new tips on prospecting.

As a bonus, I bet you'll learn a thing or two along the way!

Lastly, if this seems like something you're not ready for, then become a connector. Connectors are among the most valuable and appreciated people because they help provide resources to those who need them without expecting anything in return.

You can connect:

- People <> People
- People <> Things (they care about)
- People <> Events
- People <> Articles, books, blogs, podcasts

When you live with an abundance mindset and share your knowledge openly, everybody wins!

#17

BUILD YOUR OWN LEADERSHIP TRIBE

Regardless of the industry you're in, you are only as strong as the community you work in. Be a contributor in your community by joining an online Facebook group, joining a message board, or even making a group chat that focuses on management.

A lot of times these groups are a great resource for managing tips, strategies, and mindset secrets that you can implement into your daily workflow.

They're also great places to build a sense of community because no matter what pain points or stressors you're dealing with, these groups give you a place with people in similar positions to bounce ideas off of. In addition to online communities, build your own managing tribe at your organization.

Get with other managers at your company that want to level up their leadership abilities.

You can have regular get-togethers where you troubleshoot problems, share hacks and secrets, and read and discuss books on management and leadership.

Build your own leadership tribe and look to it to uplift one another.

#18

YOU CAN ALWAYS LEARN SOMETHING NEW TO DO BETTER

A great leader knows how much they still have to learn, even when they are considered an expert by their team or by others in their network.

A bad leader, on the other hand, wants to be considered an expert and cherished by others around them before they have even learned enough to know how little they know.

Be a great leader and recognize that there's always room for improvement.

#19
BREAK THE RULES

We all have been trained from an early age to follow the rules.

School, family, society as a whole—you name it. Everyone is always telling us to stay inside the box and stick to the rules.

A lot of rules exist for our best interests, and they keep us safe. And as a manager, you probably look to rules to create some sense of focus and structure. However, if you want to become the top leader at your organization, you have to learn when to break the rules.

Instead of sticking to the rules until they become irrelevant, true leaders follow the rules until they find a more optimum way to do things.

When it comes to the rules, instead of saying, "That's just the way things are," always ask yourself, "How can we do this better?"

Asking this question will help you break the rules and come up with new ones when it's time to do so.

#20
LEARN WHEN TO BEST
USE YOUR TIME

It doesn't matter who you are. We get only 24 hours in a day.

The difference between mediocre managers and leaders is that the latter make the most out of those 24 hours. And one of the tricks to making the most out of your time is playing to your strengths.

If you're an early riser, play to that strength and get the most difficult tasks done in the early morning hours. If you're more of a night person, your brain is at its sharpest at night. Play to that strength and leave your hardest work for the nighttime.

Whatever your peak time is, I want you to remember that time waits for no one, so make sure you know your strengths and when you're performing at your best. Then play to that strength and get your greatest work done at those peak hours.

#21
NEVER BE AN ENTITLED LEADER

No one owes you anything. Your past successes are just that—a thing of history.

So instead of dwelling on the past, obsess over what value you are delivering today for your team. What are you going to do today to maximize your team's results and grow the business?

Never let the past turn you into an entitled leader.

#22
STRENGTH VS. WEAKNESS

Teach the difference between strength and weakness.

Admitting your mistakes and taking ownership = strength.
Not taking responsibility = weakness.

Strong performers admit when they're wrong.

Be strong.

#23

MAKE IT THEIR IDEA RATHER THAN YOURS

Whenever you have a brilliant idea, instead of taking ownership of the idea and making it your own, share the concept with your team. This way when you see the idea come to fruition, everyone can take ownership of the win.

#24

HELP YOUR PEOPLE FEEL SAFE

Create an environment where people feel safe to be themselves, to think outside the box, and to take action without fear of failure.

One of the top things I try to do as a leader is make the people around me feel safe because safety creates speed and autonomy in business. When people aren't stressed thinking about whether they're going to lose their job if they take risks, they're able to come up with their greatest ideas.

When people feel secure, they can execute at full force. The entire business moves faster and produces greater results in a shorter time span as a result.

Help your people feel safe.

#25

PAY MORE ATTENTION TO WHAT PEOPLE DO, NOT WHAT THEY SAY

If you're just starting out in a management role at a new organization, you want to focus more on what is actually getting done, not what people tell you.

People will always tell you what sounds good, but they won't tell you about the bottleneck pains the company has had for months, unspoken priorities, or how to successfully collaborate with your team. These are all things you have to observe on your own.

Get into the habit of paying close attention to what people do and ask the right questions:

- What are deemed successes and failures? How is this measured?
- How do my team's goals align with the company's larger goals?
- Who are the key stakeholders?

When you ask the right questions and make constant observations, you're going to quickly pick up on what your company sees as valuable and where you can make much-needed contributions.

#26

IF YOU BRING VALUE TO YOUR TEAM, YOU WILL BE VALUED

Figure out what would be valued by the team most to be successful and then go do just that.

Get a sense of what the priorities are and what the organization deems important and valuable, and frame your workflow around that information.

#27

DON'T EXPECT YOUR TEAM
TO WORK HARDER THAN YOU

As the leader or manager, people will always expect you to be the hardest worker in the room. As a leader or manager, it's crazy to expect your employees to work as hard or as much as you do.

It's your team that you have to manage after all. Your success and your reputation are all dependent on the success of the team. With so much at stake, you will always naturally be more passionate about the success of the team, and you will always work harder than your employees.

They don't have as big of an investment, and they just don't love it as much as you do. . .or at least not yet.

When you go all-in and own your responsibility as a leader to be the hardest worker in the room, you can truly help your team maximize their potential, build stronger relationships, and have much more successful interactions.

By setting the right expectations with your team and with yourself as the leader, you can accomplish anything.

#28

TEACH YOUR TEAM TO INVEST
IN THEIR OWN SELF-DEVELOPMENT

Every dollar you invest in your own personal self-development will return a $10 investment in some form or fashion in the future.

The best reason to invest in self-improvement is that no one else is going to do it for you.

Investing in your own self-development can span many forms:

- Reading books daily
- Taking courses on subjects you need to improve on or want to master
- Joining masterminds
- Getting mentors
- Studying peers and bosses
- Transforming your mindset and daily habits for the better

Teach your team that when they aren't working, they should invest in improving themselves. Then the compounding interest and returns to their success will be unstoppable.

#29

SURROUND YOURSELF WITH THE GREATEST TALENT

The people you surround yourself with will impact you, for better or worse, more than any self-help book ever could.

With this in mind, you want to take a look at your surroundings and level up the people around you: your team, your friends, and your peers.

When you level up your circle, you level up your knowledge and wisdom.

#30

BECOME THE LEADER YOU WISHED YOU HAD

Write down all the things you loved about the great leaders you worked for, and write down all the things you hated about the bad leaders you worked for.

Work hard to multiply the things you loved about the greatest leaders you've had. And work hard to avoid doing the things you hated about the worst leaders you've had.

Never stop striving to become the leader you wish you'd always had.

#31

INVEST IN YOURSELF CONTINUOUSLY

People will invest in you, follow you, listen to you, and respect you as a leader when you invest in yourself.

At work, you will be replaced if you don't continuously invest in yourself. At business, you will be washed out if you stop investing in yourself. In relationships, you will become dissatisfied if you stop investing in yourself.

- Upgrade your professional operating system.
- Unlearn the wrong practices. Learn the new best practices.
- Upgrade and upskill just like you upgrade your gadgets.

The team will keep you only if you keep replacing yourself with a newer, better version.

MONTH 12

DEVELOPING FUTURE LEADERS, COACHING, AND SUCCESSION PLANNING

#1

EVERY EMPLOYEE IS A DIAMOND IN THE ROUGH

Not everyone on your team is going to be a rock star, but the way that you get your people to become the best versions of themselves is by looking at every employee as the next great superstar at your organization.

What happens time and time again when you take this approach is that the employee ends up living up to your initial expectations, and they actually do become a rock star.

This always happens because when you see your employees as diamonds in the rough, you start treating them as such, giving them expert guidance and creating a space where they can take risks and push themselves to grow and flourish.

So, whenever you have a new employee who comes on board, expect them to become the next great rock star at your company and focus on providing all the resources and mentorship you can provide to empower them to live up to your expectations.

#2

GET YOUR TEAM TO INVEST IN THEIR SUCCESS

Here's what happens when you invest in becoming the best you can be:

You get a lot better.

Your co-workers see you getting better.

They want to get better.

Your friends see you getting better.

They want to get better.

Your network sees you getting better.

They want to get better.

Your family sees you getting better.

They want to get better.

If you aren't going to invest in your success, then do it for everyone else.

#3

LEAD WITH PURPOSE RATHER THAN DESIRE

There are two types of managers:

- Those who are driven by desire:
  - To close big deals
  - To make a lot of money
  - To get their team at the top of the dashboard

- Those who are driven by purpose:
  - To maximize their employees' success
  - To serve their team
  - To help their customers
  - To bring value to the business

Purpose is a calling, a goal higher than yourself. Purpose will always outperform desire.

So when you lead and manage others, do it with purpose.

#4

COACH YOUR MANAGERS TO BECOME GREAT LEADERS

Why do new managers perform poorly or drop the ball when it comes to coaching? Because they receive little to no training.

This is even true with experienced managers.

Most companies promote their A players and best performers to top management positions. Then, because this top talent was never taught or trained on how to lead, they wing it, and their team suffers as a consequence. If you are hiring or promoting anyone to management, make sure they have the training required to be successful. Don't just assume that because they are amazing at their role, they will automatically be able to transfer those skills and talents to a team.

Don't let your new leaders fail the future leaders of tomorrow.

#5

BREAK FREE FROM MICROMANAGEMENT

There are two types of leaders in the business world: micromanagers and leaders.

Micromanagers:

- Fear that if they give up control their team will crash and burn
- Are obsessed with quota to the point that all they do is run numbers and hound their employees if they are behind on quota
- Kill employees' passion for their work
- Put the burden of improvement on the employee

Example: "I don't care if you have to pick up some reading, sit in on calls, or what, but you need to get better with your discovery."

Meanwhile, leaders go all-in and:

- Trust the talent, the intelligence, and the capabilities of their people
- Empower their people to maximize their potential and their creativity
- Figure out what support they can provide to set employees up for success

Example: "I noticed you've fallen behind a bit, let's look back at a couple of your calls to figure out areas of improvement."

Know the difference between a micromanager and a leader, and work to be the kind of leader who helps your people transform their careers forever and for the better.

#6

USE THESE THREE KEY FACTORS TO SPOT A POTENTIAL LEADER

It's crucial to get your exceptional employees on track to leadership positions. But how exactly do you spot those employees with leadership potential?

You want to avoid cherry-picking people who are just like you (as far as experience, etc. go) because your organization will miss out on diversity at leadership levels.

Instead, spot the potential leaders on your team with objectively by looking at these three key factors:

- Leadership abilities
- Performance history
- Company culture expertise

Look for someone with leadership abilities such as ethical character, adaptability, and great communication skills. In addition to these more traditional leadership traits, you want to look for employees who can independently problem-solve in situations where it's unclear what direction to take.

Of the three factors, an employee's performance history will tell you the most about how they would operate as a leader. If they consistently perform at the top-tier level, then they likely have what it takes or can be trained into taking on a higher position.

Lastly, expertise in company culture means not only knowing the company history but also demonstrating company values every day in their actions.

So when you're looking for potential leaders on your team, measure them against these three key factors, and that will let you know just how prepared they are to be a leader.

#7

GET OBSESSED WITH BECOMING A WORLD-CLASS COACH

A coaching agenda that helps employees constantly level up includes the following:

- **Anonymous employee assessments:** Bi-weekly, quarterly, monthly—whatever you find is appropriate for your team
- **Regular one-on-ones:** Bi-weekly (or whatever pacing you find appropriate) meetings where you cover progress on projects and goals and help your teammate with any "stuck-ons"
- **Individual stretch plans:** Plans that help each employee work through pain points identified during assessment and stretch their skills beyond what their current position requires

As you're creating a coaching agenda, you should make it clear to the employee that the goals on the agenda aren't tasks or busywork that you're asking them to complete. These are goals that they need to own and take responsibility for. Either they can meet their goals and become a better version of themselves or they can fail to meet their goals and stay stuck in the same position with the same skill set. But whatever the outcome is of their coaching agenda, you need to remind them that they're 100% responsible.

Once you complete assessments and work out stretch plans for each of your employees, you should work every day to help your people meet the goals in their stretch plans so that they are consistently growing.

#8
RUN COACHING SESSIONS THAT LEAVE EMPLOYEES EMPOWERED

Here are just a few guiding principles you'll want to follow when you have your coaching sessions:

- The first rule is to keep lessons simple. When you're coming up with a lesson plan, focus on only one skill per lesson. This way you can do a deep dive with your employees.
- Another rule to follow is to eliminate the stakes of your sessions. In other words, don't use sessions as opportunities to ridicule employees and pick apart everything they're doing wrong. Always uplift your people.
- The last rule is to never forget that repetition is your friend. Whatever you've learned in life, it's because you repeated the same thing over and over until it became second nature. Take this same approach to your coaching. Start a session with a specific skill. Demonstrate the skill and have your people break up into pairs and repeat the same skills. And repeat the lessons because they often won't stick the first time.

Follow these guidelines, and when employees leave your sessions, they're going to feel so empowered with the tips you shared, they'll be ready to run through a wall and crush every single goal!

#9

MAKE THE MOST OF YOUR TOP TALENT BEFORE THEY GO SOMEWHERE ELSE

When you discover top talent at your organization, you want to get them on track to leadership positions as soon as possible.

The days when an exceptional employee would stay at a company through retirement and become an invaluable asset over a decades-long career are all but gone. Today, exceptionally talented employees will make a number of job changes throughout their lifetime as better opportunities come up.

Instead of working against this fact, work with it and give your employees a reason to want to stick around. Give your people stretch projects where they are challenged to exercise those natural leadership abilities. Promote people to higher positions.

Truly dynamic leadership is rare. When you find someone with that "It" factor, help them start harnessing that talent for the sake of their career and your company.

#10

EVEN IF YOU OUTSOURCE TRAINING, EXECUTING COACHING IS YOUR JOB

There are many benefits to coaching your own team.

Hands-on training builds trust, and it helps you get an accurate sense of your team's strengths and weaknesses.

However, if hands-on training isn't an option and your company outsources its trainers, this secret is a reminder that you still have to make sure your people are not only mastering the training sessions but applying what they learn.

It doesn't matter how amazing the trainers are, your team is your responsibility.

Once that trainer leaves, the odds of your employees retaining anything they covered are low, so it's your job to make sure the lessons stick. You can ensure that your people are getting the most value out of coaching sessions by supplementing them with your own.

You want to be a dependable resource for your employees if they have questions. And integrate the lessons the external coach covers in daily stand-ups, one-on-ones, and group sessions.

#11

USE DATA TO PRIORITIZE COACHING

When you are working with each person on your team, leverage data to tell you which area of training and development will have the greatest results and positive impact on someone's success that month.

Personalize the training and development plan to that specific area of development.

This will help you accurately figure out the top priorities in your coaching plans for every employee.

#12

INCREASE YOUR COACHING TIME

If you're in sales, with this secret I urge you to increase your sales coaching time.

The average sales leader isn't coaching anywhere near as much as they should because their priorities are everywhere else. But coaching should be your number-one priority because it's the biggest proven ROI driver for any sales team.

Think about it: if your team's responsibility is to sell your products and services, you're going to 10× or 100× their results by training your team on how to do effective discovery, how to handle every objection with ease, and how to drive relevant value to every prospect.

Instead of focusing on bureaucratic leadership work, spend more time doing group role play, pulse checks, sales call reviews, and workshops. And whatever your schedule looks like right now, you should spend the majority (more than 50%) of your day and your week on sales training.

Putting in the hours as a coach can make the difference between someone being a mediocre sales manager and a dynamic, all-in sales leader.

More importantly, when you prioritize training, you can create an unstoppable sales team of rock stars lightning fast.

#13
TRAIN YOUR TEAM TO BE THE CEO OF THEIR BUSINESS

Work with each of your team members to think, execute, operate, and optimize like the CEO of their own business.

Never play the victim game. Assume 100% ownership for their success or failure.

Recommend extreme ownership to do whatever it takes with any team member to maximize the success of the company.

#14

UNLOCK YOUR EMPLOYEES' GREATEST MOTIVATORS

Everyone goes through stages of life where what motivated them five years ago doesn't motivate them now.

When I started my career, I just wanted to learn. In my early 20s, my goal moved from learning to becoming financially secure. Now that I am in my 30s, I cherish servant leadership and spending time with my family.

As an exercise, list the following motivators, and every year ask each team member to rank what motivates them to go to work every day, from most important to least important.

Here is the list that I use:

- Money and compensation
- Benefits
- Time off
- Learning and development
- Recognition and praise
- Career growth opportunities
- Removal of pain or problems
- Team camaraderie
- Mission to serve customers and employees

And when you think about inspiring, rewarding, and recognizing your people, always leverage this list of priorities for each individual so you know what motivates them because you can't help someone if you don't know what they want.

#15

MOTIVATE YOUR PEOPLE TO WANT TO WORK WITH PASSION

No one likes to be bossed around. When people are told what to do, their natural instinct is to push back.

So when you want something from your team, instead of barking out demands, use suggestive phrases like "Would you mind. . ." or "I hope this isn't an inconvenience but. . .." These kinds of phrases are not only polite, but they will warm up the employee to the request.

Additionally, gauge the employee's thoughts on the request:

- What do they think is the best approach to take with completing the task?
- How can the project be refined to make a bigger impact?

Even when you ask an employee to do something, if you give them ownership of the idea, they'll be willing to put in the hard work to make sure the task is done well.

#16

GIVE FEEDBACK RIGHT AWAY

Many managers will recognize an area for improvement and then wait weeks or months to share it with their employees (honestly by then they usually forget all about the feedback).

Great leaders, by contrast, give feedback as quickly as possible because the faster you can give feedback, the quicker you can help your employee break bad habits and improve.

Imagine you're the head coach for a Super Bowl championship team. As the coach, if you see your star player making a move that scores fewer touchdowns or decreases their odds of winning, you would identify and correct that losing strategy or play without hesitation because it could cause you to lose the championship game.

The same goes for your team.

If employees are shocked by the feedback they get at a performance review, then you've failed as a manager because you should never wait until quarterly reviews to provide employees with the constructive feedback they need to grow.

Simply telling someone that they need to improve without giving any specifics is merely a complaint that helps no one out. But constructive feedback includes specific strategies and recommendations on how an employee can improve.

Coaching a top team member that they are doing well but that you want to help them improve at A and strategies to help could be X, Y, Z to try. That is an example of giving great feedback.

Make sure that you give great constructive feedback to your team as quickly as possible so you can avoid any surprises when quarterly reviews roll around.

#17

MAKE YOUR MONTHLY REVIEW AN OPPORTUNITY FOR REFLECTION AND STRATEGY

Monthly reviews are similar to the bi-weekly one-on-ones in that the employee should drive the conversation.

The only difference is monthly reviews are part reflection and part quarter performance strategy. You want to give your employee the chance to think about what their big wins were in the past month.

- What progress did they make toward their quarterly goals (make sure this is quantifiable)?
- Are things moving faster or slower than they originally thought they would?
- What do they want to do over the next month to close out the quarter strong?

When someone asks you to reflect on what you've done over the past month, that can be daunting at first. So just like with the one-on-one, these are questions you can list in your calendar invite to get the employee thinking and to maximize the value out of your meeting.

These are other questions you can include:

- What have been major highs over the past month?
- What have been major lows over the past month?
- Where are you at with your quarterly KPIs? Are you ahead? Behind? Right on time?
- What next steps are you planning to take toward your quarterly goals?
- What do you need from me to help you toward your goals?

Just like you would do for your one-on-one, create a write-up of key talking points from your conversation, and share them with your employee.

#18
CONDUCT ANNUAL REVIEWS THAT FUEL GROWTH

During annual reviews with your individual contributors, pull up their annual KPI goals and notes from their previous quarterly review, and identify plans to help them grow over the next year.

Discuss:

- What went well over the past year
- What can be improved
- What I/we can do to help you win more
- What blockers were experienced

Additionally, do an annual goal review. Take a look at their:

- Professional goals
- Personal goals

The only way for you to help grow your people every year is to understand annually what each person's goals are.

One person may want to get promoted to a managerial position. Another person may hate their current role but love the company and want to switch teams. Discussing each team member's progress toward their personal and professional goals will help you better understand your employees and what they need from you.

To grow your business, you need to grow your people.

Leverage annual reviews as an important time to help maximize the growth of your teammates.

#19

FOCUS ON HIGH POTENTIALS

Identify your high-potential individual contributors on your team. And do whatever it takes to transform your high potentials into high performers.

You can have the best recruiting agency in the world, but if you don't invest in their success and develop these individuals to maximize their performance, your people will fail. So identify the gaps in knowledge, strategy, execution, culture, decision-making, and initiative.

Coach them up to fill those gaps as quickly as possible.

Investing in developing your high potentials and turning them into high performers pays long-term compounding interest that builds unstoppable teams.

#20
CREATE PROMOTION LADDERS FOR EVERY POSITION

Before you hire anyone, make it a requirement to share the promotion ladder, career track, or department-switching plans with them.

Present this to your management and present this to the candidate. Furthermore, educate your new team member that if they are in a position they don't love but they love the company, share how they can switch to different departments or divisions and work in a role that is better suited for them.

Success is a game, and every day your employees wake up striving to reach the next level. If they think they are stuck at the first level of the game, they are likely to churn.

The same goes for people who don't know how to play the game, don't know the next levels, or may be playing a game that they don't like and want to switch (such as switching departments, roles, or positions).

The more you can gamify your hired positions and make it clear to employees how to win and get promoted the more motivated your people will be to keep achieving new heights!

#21

TEACH EMPLOYEES HOW TO GET AHEAD

Future leaders don't wait for someone to tell them what to do. They get ahead by doing more than what's required.

They figure out what would move the organization forward. They anticipate the needs of the business and the customers and they go make it happen without having to be told what to do.

A leader is someone who inspires you to do more and be more. Employees who do more and achieve more without anyone telling them are the leaders of tomorrow.

If you have employees who are looking to get ahead, teach them this secret.

#22

TAKE ON THE ROLE BEFORE YOU ACTUALLY HAVE THE POSITION

Teach your employees and individual contributors to start doing the job they want in the future right now. Today.

The best way to succeed on any team or at any company is to identify where you want to be in the company a year from now. Then start being that person right now.

- Learn the things you need to learn to be the best at that future job.
- Assume the job before you have the position.
- Go the extra mile because you know you can do it.
- Be the leader in that position before you are chosen for the role.

Don't be complicit with your current job and do the bare minimum. Remind your team that when the company is ready to promote someone to the next position, anyone who makes these moves will be the first person to be considered because they've already demonstrated that they are more than prepared to do the work.

#23

DON'T WAIT TO PROMOTE

When your people are ready, promote them.

When people on your team have consistently exceeded your expectations, represented the core values of the company, and helped the people around them become the best they can be, promote them ASAP! Don't wait for an annual review.

I've promoted people I've hired as quickly as 30 days after they started because they performed above and beyond the job requirements.

Most companies will promote salary increases, raises, or title changes only once a year (if that. . .). But if you have a game changer on the team, a competitor will try to hire them.

So, promote your people when they are ready and don't wait. It's only going to help you and the team accelerate your path to hitting goals.

#24

BE INTENTIONAL WITH YOUR COMPLIMENTS

You should always be the first to give praise to your people when they win.

However, if you want to make the biggest impact, stay away from vague compliments. The more specific you can get with your praise, the better.

The reason you don't want to use generic compliments like "Well done!" or "Great work!" is because these vague statements sound fake and insincere.

It comes across like you're saying something nice because you have to, not because you genuinely mean it.

So next time you want to pay a compliment, make specific observations, like "Your follow-up was consistent! And you found a great balance between being persistent without being annoying." Or, "Excellent objection handling!"

This type of impactful feedback is the reinforcement your employees need to continue to win.

#25

ANYTIME SOMEONE GETS PROMOTED, PERSONALLY CALL THEM TO CONGRATULATE THEM

When an employee gets promoted, make a point to call them up and congratulate them.

Tell them how much you appreciate them and how grateful you are for all of their hard work. Congratulate them on their professional success thus far, and let them know that you don't take their contributions to the company for granted.

Lastly, close out by asking your newly promoted team member what you can help them with to maximize their success in the new role. If there is anything they have questions, concerns, or doubts about, work to get them addressed so they hit the ground running!

#26

ASK THE TEAM, "WHAT DID YOU LEARN TODAY?"

In your daily standups and one-on-ones, instead of asking your employees, "How was your day?" ask, "What did you learn today?"

The key to building an unstoppable team is to instill the value of constant growth.

Asking and sharing something new every day will remind your team to keep this principle at the forefront of their workday. Sharing what each of your team members learns every day can increase the wisdom of the group. Additionally, asking "What did you learn?" is going to elicit more retrospective answers beyond "Good" or "OK" (which is what you get with "How was your day?"). To answer "What did you learn today?" you have to really think about what impacted you positively that can help others.

I personally updated our one-on-ones to include this question in both our daily standups and our review cycles. I hope it helps you too if you decide to do the same.

#27

GET A PROGRESS PARTNER

When you're leading your team, day in and day out, after a while you can start to lose sight of ways you can improve. This is why with this secret, I urge you to get a progress partner.

Think of a progress partner as someone who can hold you accountable for your growth. A progress partner can spot weak areas and help you further improve your natural strengths.

You can, in turn, give your progress partner the same feedback.

As far as selecting a progress partner, choose a colleague:

- **Who is on your same level:** Don't pick someone above or below you in terms of your company's hierarchy because they may not be equipped to assess you properly.
- **Who you get along with:** They need to understand and mesh well with your personality.
- **Who you trust:** Choose someone who you know is going to be constructive (rather than destructive) with their feedback.

When you pick a progress partner, discuss what your goals are.

- Are there particular areas that you need to work on?
- Are there upcoming projects that you would like to be held accountable for?

Once you settle your goals, do regular check-ins. Whether you check in weekly or monthly, make the meetings a quick casual phone call or coffee meeting; that way they're low risk, and you're not likely to bail on them.

If you want to constantly improve, consider getting a progress partner because they will help you become a stronger, more productive, and efficient manager.

#28
YOU ARE NEVER TOO IMPORTANT

You are never too important to be nice to your people.

You are never too important to appreciate your people.

You are never too important to learn from your people.

You are never too important to care about the success of your people.

#29
YOU ARE IN CONTROL

Coach your people that they are in control of their success and their failure.

You will never control your future if you let your present be controlled by your past. So step up and own your responsibilities. Step up and own your future success. Take extreme ownership and full responsibility for everything good and bad in your life.

When you take extreme ownership of your life, you are 100% in control.

#30
SPEAK SUCCESS INTO EXISTENCE

Whatever you want in life, you have to speak it into existence. A promotion, a new car, a big beautiful house—you name it. With any kind of success, if you believe it, you will achieve it.

This mindset is usually applied to your personal and professional life, but it's also a fundamental managing secret that you can apply to your employees. If you have nothing but great things to say about an employee, their abilities, and everything they can achieve, you speak their success into existence. When you talk up an employee, they will go out of their way to live up to the amazing things you said about them.

On the flip side, if you have an employee who is underperforming or is weak in a particular area, talk them up and brag about them as if they mastered that weak area. This attention will motivate them to work harder and prove you right.

Speak success into existence not only for yourself, but for your team and your future.

Conclusion

"There's no better feeling in the world than helping your team become the best they can be.

Going all-in is a marathon, not a sprint.

Work on it every day and never give up!

You can accomplish anything if you're All-in, Always, in All Ways!"
—Brandon Bornancin

I hope *The Power of Going All-In* gave you everything you need to become the best leader you can be, both professionally and personally.

I've shared a number of strategies with you, from servant leadership to radical transparency, and I hope that these secrets not only help you maximize your potential but that your team's performance skyrockets!

So, what's next for you on your all-in leadership journey?

As you already know, the greatest leaders always put in the hard work, rain or shine, because all-in leadership requires nothing less than 100% effort day in and day out.

In that spirit of continuous improvement, I highly recommend re-reading this book because with new levels of success come new challenges. Throughout your career as you re-read this book, you will bring new perspectives. And this book, in turn, will give you ideas and strategies you hadn't considered before. You'll truly be surprised by the insights you gain reading this book a second time around!

Last but not least, I want to congratulate you on mastering *The Power of Going All-In*! I can't wait to follow your continued journey and see everything you accomplish!

Your success is my success,
Brandon Bornancin
CEO & Founder
www.seamless.ai
www.brandonbornancin.com

Quick Favor to Ask Before You Go

If you like to help others without asking for anything in return, then you're my kind of people, and I have a quick favor to ask.

You see, there's someone out there right now who is right where you were when you started *The Power of Going All-In*. They're struggling with business and leadership, and they're not sure where to begin when it comes to improvement and transforming their results.

Your review can be the tipping point that wakes them up to take action, to change the trajectory of their life, and to finally invest their time and energy in a resource like this book.

Could you please take a few seconds right now to leave a review on Amazon?

Here's the link:

https://www.amazon.com/All-Leadership-Give-Everything-Succeed/dp/1394196180

The more reviews the book has, the easier it will be for others just like you to find it.

Plus, you'll feel great knowing that you helped somebody become the best person their business, their team, and their family need, which is what *The Power of Going All-In* is all about!

Lastly, if you won't do it to help others, then please do it for me. I spent years putting together this book to help people like you, and I print every review to put in my office as inspiration to keep serving my readers at the highest level.

Thank you in advance for your review; I'm eternally grateful for readers like you!

About the Author

Brandon Bornancin is the CEO and Founder of Seamless.AI, the world's best sales leads software. He's a serial entrepreneur, expert salesperson, bestselling author, and award-winning team builder.

After hiring more than 1,000 people, building a company worth more than $100,000,000, and winning countless top employer awards like "Top Places to Work," "#1 Tech Company of The Year," and "Linked-In's Top 10 Startups," Brandon knows the ins and outs of leadership from managerial, entrepreneurial, and employee perspectives.

With all this experience, Brandon has discovered the dos and don'ts of leading teams, scaling companies, and helping employees maximize their potential through the good times and the bad.

Index